Amy,

I thought of you when I came across this book. I'm sure you'll enjoy this book. Ever since I watched your knitting so well I enjoy must all our Math tutoring so well are wonderful! Thank you!

♡ Mary Lou ☺

Not Tonight Darling,
I'm Knitting

Betsy Hosegood

D&C

David and Charles

A DAVID & CHARLES BOOK
Copyright © David & Charles Limited 2006

David & Charles is an F+W Publications Inc. company
4700 East Galbraith Road
Cincinnati, OH 45236

First published in the UK in 2006

Text copyright © Betsy Hosegood 2006

A catalogue record for this book is available from the
British Library.

ISBN-13: 978-0-7153-2407-3 hardback
ISBN-10: 0-7153-2407-1 hardback

Printed in Singapore by KHL Printing Co Pte Ltd.
for David & Charles
Brunel House   Newton Abbot   Devon

Commissioning Editor Jennifer Proverbs
Assistant Editor Louise Clark
Project Editor Nicola Hodgson
Head of Design Prudence Rogers
Production Controller Ros Napper

Visit our website at www.davidandcharles.co.uk

David & Charles books are available from all good
bookshops; alternatively you can contact our Orderline
on 0870 9908222 or write to us at FREEPOST EX2 110,
D&C Direct, Newton Abbot, TQ12 4ZZ (no stamp
required UK only); US customers call 800-289-0963
and Canadian customers call 800-840-5220.

contents

Introduction   4

Knitting unravelled   **8**

Knits in history   10

The charms of yarn   18

The new knitting circles   24

Trailing yarns   **30**

Your knitting journey   32

True yarns   36

Quiz – what's your style?   46

Shop till you drop — 48

Fanciable fibres — 50

Shoppers' paradise — 54

Choices, choices — 58

What's your type? — 62

I've just gotta have it! — 68

You're in good company — 70

Taking back the knit — 72

The knitterati — 74

Knit parade — 80

Knitting inspirations — 82

The shapely '30s — 84

The war-time '40s — 88

The fabulous '50s — 90

The swinging '60s — 96

The arty '60s — 98

The hippy chic '70s — 100

The booming '80s — 102

End of a century — 106

21st-century knits — 108

Last of the yarn — 112

Aftercare — 114

Shows, groups, resources — 116

Acknowledgments — 120

Index — 121

Why not tonight, darling?

Ever since the Reverend William Lee designed the knitting frame because he thought that his wife was spending too much time with her needles (see page 13), it has been clear that knitting can become an overwhelming passion, ousting interest in all other activities and even people. Meals are left unprepared, clothes unwashed and other jobs unfinished in the overwhelming desire to knit just one more row.

So what is it about knitting that can absorb our attention so fully that it becomes no longer a hobby but a way of life? Unlike a good film, which 'can't please all of the people all of the time', knitting can be all things to all people. Most of us find it a relaxing and therapeutic exercise, helping us to unwind in moments of leisure, but if you don't want to relax you can knit your anger into it or even your enmity, like Madame Defarge in Charles Dickens' *A Tale of Two Cities*. You can knit slowly, in a relaxed, almost sleepy way, or you can knit madly and tightly, expending large amounts of energy and thereby using it as a means of burning calories.

Knitting is also about expressing your creativity. Many of us feel the need to make something with our hands from time to time, but when the urge strikes out of the blue, what do you do? Painting demands considerable skill, and so do most forms of sewing and embroidery. Even photography isn't as straightforward as it appears. Basic knitting skills, however, can be learned in a few hours, and you can complete your first scarf in an afternoon. What could be more satisfying than that?

Making something with yarn gives you the chance to express your individuality. Right now there's a bonanza of exciting yarns out there waiting to be turned into all manner of choice items (see pages 62–67). There are fluffy yarns and cuddly yarns, sparkly yarns and slippery yarns, fat yarns, thin yarns, bobbly yarns and knobbly yarns. Colours aren't just plain any more either; they are mottled, speckled, streaked and multicoloured, bright, muted, harmonious or clashing. In fact, if you can think of it, you can probably buy the yarn to make it, and if you can't, there are spinners who will make it specially for you. So if you've ever gone out to buy a specific item to finish off an outfit and come back sad and empty-handed because the exact thing you were looking for wasn't to be found, lament no more. Just knit it. Likewise, if you're one of those people who always wants something six months before it comes into the shops, turn your designer talent to good use and get knitting. By the time you've finished, you'll be bang up in fashion.

Knitting is also great for your social life. If you knit on a train or a bus, complete strangers read your knitting as a sign saying 'I'm friendly, sane and don't bite'. They will ask you what you are knitting or reminisce about knitters in their family, and before you know it, everyone around you is joining in. Knit on circular needles or with four needles 'in the round' and you'll turn even more heads. Join a knitting club (see pages 25–26) or get on a weblog and you could find yourself going out for a knitting social more times than you stay in.

Knitting is also about getting back to basics. It's fun to discover new skills on the computer, to listen to an MP3 player, take photos with our phones and get all our friends' names entered on our palms, but all that technology needs a balance, and a traditional skill like knitting is ideal. In our fast world, knitting is snail-slow, and that very slowness gives us the time we need to unwind. It's like taking a walk after driving on the motorway. At first it seems as if we're not getting anywhere and then, as we start to look around, we enjoy the pace and the journey becomes its own fulfilment. Knitting is the same. It's not just finishing a garment that counts, it's the process of getting there.

Finally, there is an immense comfort in knitting. Maybe it's because our mothers or grandmothers knitted and simply watching someone knitting is like having a hug, or maybe it's the sensation of the soft yarn slipping between our fingers or the slow but inevitable progression from row to row. Perhaps it's the miracle of growth as the knitting transforms from that first stitch, then first row into its budding potential and finally blossoms as a finished garment. Whatever it is, it's wonderful.

> "A well-made sweater, knitted with good will and good wool, is beyond price.
>
> Elizabeth Zimmermann

Knitting
unravelled

Knits in history

Retro fashion, and retro knitwear in particular, is highly fashionable these days. But how far back in history do you want to go to get inspiration for your craft and for your personal style? Knitting has a very long and venerable tradition. No one knows for sure who first picked up the first knitting needles, or when, but wise people have known for centuries what a satisfying craft it is.

You don't need to know anything about the origins of knitting to enjoy this creative, inspiring and therapeutic activity – which is just as well, because nobody really knows when and where it all started. Like needlework, knitting seems to have been around forever. If fourteenth-century Italian and German artists are to be believed, the Virgin Mary was a keen exponent of the craft, favouring four or five needles and working in the round with multiple threads of different colours – obviously she was experienced and highly skilled. But guess what the earliest piece of surviving knitting is. Do you think it might be an elegant lady's chemise or a knight's robe? I'm afraid not. The earliest surviving items that we can be certain were handknitted are blue and white cotton socks, much like those blue and white terry-towelling numbers that are such favourites on the beach when worn with sturdy sandals. These items date back to somewhere around 1300 AD in Egypt. If all modern knitting was derived from those socks then the craft has obviously come a long way.

In Medieval Europe, the average upper-class male besported himself in rather natty hose (tights to you and me) that had been handknitted in a colour bright enough to draw the eye of any passing damsel and perhaps incur the jealousy of fellow males. He might also have worn a knitted hat, which was another popular item. Knitted stockings were a favourite for many years, and by the late 1500s, when Elizabeth I was queen, England was the leading stocking exporter, which meant the nation's poor had a means to supplement their meagre incomes.

> *You don't need to know about the origins of knitting to enjoy this creative, inspiring and therapeutic activity*

RIGHT: Women of leisure sit in their basket chairs knitting, on the balcony overlooking the River Thames, London.

Ladylike looks
In Victorian times, it was fashionable for ladies to hold their needles between thumb, forefinger and second finger, rather like a pencil. It was much slower than the traditional method of holding the needles under the hands, but then, when one was a lady, speed was not as important as one's appearance.

However, just when things were going swimmingly for handknitting – or perhaps because of it – a vicar by the name of William Lee (1563/4–c. 1614) went and invented the knitting frame in 1589. The story goes that his lady fair was spending so much time knitting that he was stirred to jealousy of those flashing needles and invented a machine to do the job instead, leaving her free to minister to him. He duly went to see the queen about getting a patent, but Elizabeth I felt that the resulting knitting was too coarse and wanted to protect the handknitting industry, so she turned it down. Not to be put off, our ardent lover popped over to France and set up a business over there. Unfortunately, the French king, Henry IV, was assassinated, which slowed matters up for Lee, and the potential of his invention wasn't fully realized until after his death. Presumably Lee's lady went on handknitting to the end, so I guess there's a happy ending there…

The knitting frame ultimately led to the demise of handknitting as a commercial venture, but

LEFT: Knitting has always been a convivial activity – you can knit and chat at the same time.

William Lee was stirred to jealousy of those flashing knitting needles and invented a machine to do the job instead

because it was cheaper to knit garments than to buy them, it continued as an activity in the home. During the World Wars it was encouraged for the greater good, and women were asked to contribute to the war effort by knitting for the troops. Afterwards, things were never the same. Women had had a chance to do men's work and wanted to carry on; domestic activities, such as knitting and cooking, rather went out of fashion. It was left to yarn manufacturers, designers and the likes of Elizabeth Zimmermann (see page 14) to put creativity and inventiveness back into the frame.

Marked men
British knitters in fishing communities of old used patterns of cables to produce dense sweaters to keep their menfolk warm at sea. But the sweaters had another, more macabre, purpose. Each family used unique patterns in their Guernseys (or Ganseys) so that should an accident befall the man, his body could be identified even after the sea had done its worst.

The yarn goddesses

Forty years ago, knitting was dead as far as most people were concerned – it was considered a staid hobby for the elderly who seemed capable of making only repulsive sweaters, bootees and over-ornate baby clothes. So what happened? What motivated yarn producers to create the gorgeous and funky creations we see on yarn store shelves, and why are knitting patterns suddenly so stylish, wearable and appealing?

The first thing that happened was Elizabeth Zimmermann. Born in England, but living in the US, she was the Martha Stewart or Delia Smith of knitting, bringing it to the masses and making everyone feel that they could do it. In her books, classes, TV and radio appearances, Mrs Zimmermann explained how knitting could be done easily and efficiently and, above all, with humour. At first the editors of her magazine articles edited out her personal voice and her sense of humour, but in the end they let it shine through; reading her books is like having a chat with a very witty neighbour who happens to be an expert on knitting too.

> *Reading Mrs Zimmermann's books is like chatting to a witty neighbour who happens to be an expert on knitting*

Not many young knitters have heard of Elizabeth Zimmermann, but her influence has survived because she inspired so many knitting designers, including Kaffe Fassett (legendary for his

Mrs Zimmermann
Elizabeth Zimmermann (1910–1999) was born in England, educated in Switzerland and settled in the US, so we can all lay claim to her. She was a voracious knitter. She knitted everywhere – even on the back of her husband's motorbike while he was driving it and in the car (as a passenger) in the dark. She wrote three books that contain very simple patterns that the reader can knit up in his or her own way, and her advice throughout is both useful and funny. These books are: *Knitting Without Tears* (basics), *Knitter's Almanac* (projects for every month) and *Knitting Around* (a series of lessons).

extraordinary use of colour). He corresponded with Mrs Zimmermann, and learnt from her the joys of circular needles. However, it was her indomitable, loveable character that had the most impact because, as Kaffe Fassett said, Mrs Zimmermann gave modern knitwear designers 'licence to be chatty, and to be informal – and funny'.

A major influence on knitting today has been the endorsement of celebrity knitters (see pages 74–79). Whether we love them or hate them, we know that if it's okay for the rich and famous to knit then it's okay for us, too. Before celebrity knitters, the craft was held in low regard because of its links with dowdy domesticity. Now that stars such as Uma Thurman and Cameron Diaz have picked up the needles, knitting has had a much-needed makeover – these glamorous modern icons are certainly not dowdy.

The interest of the young in knitting, fuelled by celebrities, has in turn fired the imagination of yarn manufacturers and pattern designers. As the variety of yarns and patterns increases, the interest in knitting goes up simply because there's something inspiring to knit with. Greater demand fuels greater production, and it seems there are newer, more exciting yarns and patterns coming on the market every day. Now there's no going back.

Celebrity knitting is not a new phenomenon – Hollywood stars such as Gloria Stuart (right) knitted on set to fill the time between shooting scenes

Knitting on the net

The move in knitting circles towards the informal and the chatty has been helped along no end by the Internet, which is such a rapid means of communication that it encourages a type of street-talk language analogous to text messaging that is constantly evolving. Indeed, there's a secret world of knitting codes, conveyed only to the initiated by a series of abbreviations, such as TOAD and SEX (see right). The Internet is also responsible for hosting knitting blogs, which enable us to learn about how other knitters live and knit (see page 38). Through these blogs we see the real side of knitting and knitaholics, and can share the knitter's triumphs and disasters, obtain advice and make friends. Many bloggers publish their own patterns for free, and many of them put up galleries of their FOs (Finished Objects). Start browsing for inspiration and information, and you'll soon realize what a keen community of yarn enthusiasts is out there.

Unravelling knit code

If you look up a knitblog on the net, these are some of the abbreviations you may come across:

EZ
Elizabeth Zimmermann (such is her influence that she has her own abbreviation)

FO
finished object

KAT
knitting against time

KIP
knitting in public

LYS
local yarn store

NQBE
not quite big enough

SEX
stash enrichment expedition (shopping for yarn)

SNB
Stitch 'n' Bitch

TOAD
trashed object, abandoned in disgust

UFO
unfinished object

USO
unstarted object

WCZ
wool-contaminated zone (yarn stash)

WIP
work in progress

YAQ
yarn acquisition quest (a variation on SEX)

The charms of yarn

Does a knitter really need to justify herself? Well, judging by the mass of books, magazine articles and blogs that proclaim the many benefits of knitting, she does. Personally, I like to knit, and that's that, but if you need a reason to indulge or have an unhelpful partner who is jealous of your knitting (and do you really want to be with someone who hates knitting?) then here are some excellent reasons to get clicking.

Unleash your creativity

Nearly all women and many men have the urge to unleash the artist within and make something so that they can say with pride 'I did that'. You may not be satisfied with your efforts with a pen or a brush and you may not be able to sew up a seam or embroider a flower, but the good news is that everybody can knit – especially, as Elizabeth Zimmermann said, 'people of superior intelligence like ourselves'. The other piece of good news is that you don't have to make any artistic decisions to feel the tremendous satisfaction of creativity. All you have to do is find a pattern that you like and start knitting. Whether you copy the pattern exactly as instructed or make your own version (either deliberately or by mistake) is immaterial. Your piece is special because you knitted your thoughts and dreams into it. Oddly enough, years afterwards, when you go to put on the item you knitted you can often pick up some of the feelings you experienced while you knitted it. Knitting an item, however small, is something that you'll never regret.

Your piece is special because you knitted your thoughts and dreams into it

Going places

Knitting is very manoeuvrable and is easy to pick up and put down. Unlike a good book, it doesn't take up all your concentration, so you can talk and knit at the same time. Unlike painting, you can do it in any weather conditions, knowing that extreme heat, cold or damp won't affect your materials, and you won't need a supply of clean water. Unlike embroidery, you can do it in poor lighting or if you have bad eyesight. And, unlike just about any other hobby, you can do it in the kitchen while watching the vegetables boil or the meat roast and you won't burn the food. You can also work in any time bytes from a few seconds to a few hours – even if you only work two stitches at a time, you've still made progress.

Knitting heals

Studies in the US have shown that doing something repetitive (like knitting) while undergoing a trauma helps you recover from the event much more quickly and easily. The problem is that you won't know when trauma is going to strike, so my advice is to knit at all times, just in case.

The glamour girls

Yes, it's true, you can knit and be glamorous. Look
at Madonna, knitting baby clothes on set, or Geri
Halliwell, knitting in her tiny bikini top and looking
oh-so-approachable in consequence.

Productive pleasure

Do you need to feel that you've achieved something
at the end of the day or sometimes feel worthless and
low? Knitting can help – knit as little as two or three
rows a day and you're a success because you've
done something productive. Buy a chunky wool such
as Point Five from Colinette and you can make a
fabulously funky scarf or hat in a few hours.

Sociable stitching

Knitting is great for your social life – yes, really. Just try to knit in public without someone coming up to you and commenting on what you are doing. Even in major cities it can't be done – except possibly in New York, where nobody notices anything. Get along to a knitting group to meet like-minded knitters or see if there is a yarn café near you (see pages 18–21). If necessary, start your own group.

Knit your nerves away

Knitting has been shown to lower blood pressure and relax mind and body. Next time you know you are going to be in a stressful situation, try taking your knitting along. Knitting in the dentist's waiting room, for example, will help soothe your nerves, while knitting before an exam will not only keep you calm but could help you achieve better results by increasing your powers of concentration (see page 23).

Boost your brainpower

Dr Robert Friedland, associate professor of neurology at the Case Western Reserve University School of Medicine in Cleveland, Ohio, has found that adults who exercised their brains in their younger years with hobbies such as knitting were 2.5 times less likely to suffer from Alzheimer's disease than those who did not.

Knit in the dentist's waiting room to soothe your nerves...

Guilt-free time

As many of us are so busy, and have a packed schedule every day, a lot of us feel hugely guilty simply sitting down to watch a favourite TV programme. If you have your knitting in your hand, you are not being a couch potato, you are being a productive knitter, so enjoy the show.

The way of knit

Knitting has been likened to yoga because it focuses the mind on a physical task rather than on any worries. It also has a meditative quality. The simplest meditation exercises usually require you to sit comfortably and count your breathing. Knitting also involves counting when you are working a pattern, and of course, you are usually sitting comfortably. In meditation the idea is not to shut out all thoughts but to allow them to pass through the mind rather than lingering. Knitting enables you to let go of unwanted thoughts because it regularly calls your attention back to the soothing occupation of knit and purl and the completion of row after row after row. Indeed, tests have shown that knitting moves the mind into the same alpha-wave pattern as meditation, and for some people knitting does this more quickly and readily.

Jailbird knits

It's not just Martha Stewart who knits in prison these days. Inmates at the Stirling Correctional Facility in the US have knitted hundreds of chemo caps for cancer patients who have lost their hair. At Jackson Correctional Institution, Wisconsin, and in other prisons in the US, inmates have been knitting items for underprivileged families and other good causes. Some prisons have encouraged inmates to knit not just as a means of making a contribution to the community but as a component of their anger-management programs.

Yarn therapy

There are many curative claims for knitting, as there probably are for other creative hobbies, but it seems particularly good for reducing nerves and stress. People who suffer from panic attacks have found it to be a cure or an alleviator, and others claim that knitting has helped them stop smoking, lose weight or deal with loss. After 9/11, yarn stores across the US noticed a dramatic rise in sales as people took up creative crafts to work through their pain. Actress Goldie Hawn announced that she was knitting a star-spangled banner as a means of mentally knitting the country back together. Other crafters followed suit, knitting or stitching a memorial to the event.

Pupil power

A few years ago, the authorities in northern India banned teachers from knitting in school on the grounds that it gave the impression that teachers weren't giving their work their full attention (see page 76). Now schools in the US, including the Manhattan Centre for Science and Mathematics, are actively encouraging pupils to knit in class because they have discovered that it aids concentration. Pupils can sit with paper and pen to the side, and stop their knitting every so often to make a note or ask a question about the topic of the lesson. No doubt pupils are also quieter because if they are occupied with knitting and trying to listen to the lesson at the same time there won't be much room left in their heads for other things.

Schools are actively encouraging pupils to knit in class as it aids concentration

The new knitting circles

You know how it feels when you just have to knit – it's good for you, both mentally and physically, as well as being a means of glamming up your wardrobe. Whether you do it alone, with your girlfriends or in public, it just always feels so darn good! Here are just a few of the places where knitters are getting their needles out.

Home is where the knit is

There's no doubting that your friends and family know you knit – you love to do it everywhere and make no secret of it. In the home, it's one of the most relaxing things you can do – it's so decadent to kick off your heels, take the phone off the hook, curl up on the sofa in front of the TV and get knitting. But be warned, some may object to the amount of time you put into your favourite hobby. My young son regards my knitting with the same kind of dislike as the cat – both take up my lap and my attention. But you may already have family members who share the highs and lows – after all, the family that knits together stays together.

Or do you prefer to get out there and share your passion with complete strangers (although, as you know, strangers are only people you haven't knitted with yet)? Since about 30% of American and British women knit these days, it shouldn't be hard to find likeminded knitting fanatics to get together with. So if you want to mingle, where should you go?

It's so decadent to kick off your heels, take the phone off the hook... and get knitting

Come together

If you prefer to craft in company, knitting groups are the way to do it. But don't worry – knitting circles these days are not just for genteel old ladies. They involve sociability with some stitching thrown in for good measure. Make new friends, learn from the other members, and share patterns, tips and even yarns. If your jumper doesn't come out in your size, maybe it will fit one of them. A group also keeps you updated and inspired on the latest events, developments and products. There are people out there knitting just about everything from fur coats and Peruvian-style phone covers to blindfolds, armchairs, pieces of modern art and knapsacks. But for all this edginess, knitting groups don't compromise on life's luxuries. Your group's favourite meeting place may be a coffee shop or wine bar. This is knitting at it's best – a glass of wine, some gossip, and a great night out.

This is knitting at it's best – a glass of wine, some gossip, and a great night out.

Knitting in public

You don't need a permit to knit in public, so you can knit anywhere that you feel comfortable – on the subway, on the bus, the train, in the park, on the beach, or wherever you like. However, it is often most enjoyable to knit in company. If you don't fancy joining a knitting group or if you want an additional venue, look out for some of the more unusual knitting events and meetings in your area. These can be sourced on the Internet, or through local newspapers, adverts and word of mouth.

One example to look out for is a film knit. Certain cinemas have special screenings at which you can watch the latest releases with the lights on so you can see your knitting at the same time. If you have a cinema like this near you, then this is also a great place to track down like-minded knitters and possibly source a local group. Other places and events to try include knit cafés, knit-outs and knit-ins.

> *The knit café Knit New York has a weekly 'Boyz Nite' to encourage their male clients to feel at home*

Knit cafés

This brilliant idea is sweeping through the US and Europe – although not fast enough for my liking. These are yarn stores that provide an area for people to knit in and may supply coffee and nibbles as well. The idea is to create a homely place where people can be comfortable, knit a bit, give or receive knitting advice and hopefully be encouraged to stay longer and buy some yarn. These are a haven for all sorts of knitters. The café Knit New York even has a weekly 'Boyz Nite' to encourage their male clients to feel at home in what is still mainly a female arena.

Knit-outs

A knit-out is an outdoor gathering of knitters. The Craft Yarn Council of America held the first knit-out at the end of the 1990s, and since then the event has grown exponentially. The 2004 event in New York's Union Square Park was attended by an amazing 30,000 knitters. They came to knit and commune with fellow knitters, to learn from the free lessons, see the shows and demonstrations and salivate over the yarn displays and designs. Another regular knit-out is held in Washington, D.C.

Knit-ins

Knit-ins are more radical than knit-outs. Cast Off is a London-based group famed for holding a knit-in on the Circle Line of the subway a few years ago and for being thrown out of the very grand Savoy Hotel for knitting. They knit in public as a statement and to 'challenge what is seen as nerdy'. They show that it's okay to knit and to encourage anyone to have a go. They show that knitting can be fun and even radical – it isn't just for grandmothers any more.

You don't need a permit to knit in public, so you can knit anywhere you feel comfortable...

Cyberknitting

The Internet is a wonderful source of yarns, free patterns and advice. You could go mad when you discover just how much is out there. However, you should use the Internet wisely and support your local yarn shop as much as possible – when it comes to choosing yarn, nothing beats the hands-on approach (see page 54). By the way, whoever said that the computer would cut down on paper hadn't counted on all the fabulous free knitting patterns out there just calling out to be downloaded and printed out. You can also buy downloadable versions of some of the latest patterns from around the world so you can have them in an instant.

As well as being a shopaholic's paradise, the Internet is a chat line to the world. Got a knitting problem? Go online to one of the many knitting blog sites such as *knitlist.com* and you'll get advice and support in no time. You'll also be able to see other people's WIPs (works in progress) and UFOs (unfinished objects). Indeed, when I last downloaded a pattern from knitting designer Annie Modesitt, I not only got help directly from the designer when I needed it, but was given a web address where I could show my work in progress to other knitters following the same pattern and see their versions too. What could be better than knitting companionably to the same pattern with people all over the world?

Setting up your own group

If you can't find a local knitting group that you feel comfortable with, you can always start your own. This is being done all over the world all the time, and if you keep things simple it should be a real pleasure. Get your friends and their friends to join and keep things flexible and easy-going unless you enjoy a lot of admin. Here are a few pointers to help get you started:

Choose a neutral venue such as a wine bar or a coffee house – if you meet at someone's house they may begin to feel put-upon or others may feel left out. Make sure that the proprietor is happy for you to have your meetings there and that the venue is large enough for your numbers to expand without you taking over the place.

Make sure the venue is easy to get to and fairly central, with good public transport nearby and/or cheap and readily available parking.

Arrange regular sessions on the same day every week or month so everyone knows when to turn up.

Get the word out the easy way. Setting up a mailing list on the Internet is a good idea because you can spread news of meetings and other events that might interest the group without spending hours doing it. Alternatively, you could set up a 'pass it on' system in which you ring one member who rings the next and so on. You might want to put a notice in the window of the local knitting shop too, advising other knitters of the event.

Turn up promptly to every session. Once the group has got going you don't have to do this, but initially it would be good if new arrivals can see a familiar face or at least know that they have come to the right place. (This also gives you the chance to nab the best chair and get your drink order in before a queue develops.)

Don't hassle members to come to every session. Set the club up on a drop-in basis. Then it will establish a relaxed feel and nobody will feel pressured to go.

Trailing yarns

Your knitting journey

One of the great things about knitting is that, just like life in general, it has its ups and downs, but you're always learning, discovering new experiences and having fun. If you don't have much confidence or skill yet, you probably keep it slow and simple. If you're a knitting pro, you're no doubt whizzing along and trying all kinds of tricks and stunts. Where are you on your knitting journey? Here we look at some of the main milestones; read on and see how far you dare to go.

In the beginning...

If you're just launching into your first projects, you're probably best off getting a pattern and following it exactly using a fairly chunky yarn and big needles – I wouldn't drop below 4.25mm (US 6) if I were you. Big stitches are easier to see and to pick up if you drop them. Avoid very fluffy yarns, such as mohair or eyelash yarn, because it will be difficult to see your stitches. Adopt a knitting mentor or buy a good book, such as *The Knitter's Bible* (see back cover), and learn how to cast on and off, to knit, purl and pick up dropped stitches. Those are the basics, and that's all you need to make a scarf or a bag. If you have to start a new ball, simply leave the old yarn at the end of a row and start knitting with the new one. If you want, knot the two loosely together and then tidy up when you've finished by unknotting and darning in the ends. Choose your yarn by instinct – if you are in love with it, you won't mind any time spent playing around with it.

Get ahead

Once they can knit straight, most people like to try something shaped. A hat is ideal because it's small and can make a set with your scarf. At this stage you need to learn two more things: how to increase and how to decrease. Both are easy. Oh, and unless you knit on circular needles, you'll need to stitch a seam. I would recommend the circular option because these needles are fun and your hat won't have an untidy side. They also enable you to avoid purl altogether, which is quicker. However, if you adore a pattern knitted on two needles then choose that. After all, you want to knit the best you can and the more you lust after the design the more effort you'll put in.

> *Don't do it with your brain; just let your hands take over.*
> *Kaffe Fassett*

Put some clothes on!

If you can knit a hat, your next challenge is to knit a sweater. Or you can knit a gilet, tank top, bikini or just about anything else. Along the way, your pattern may teach you some alternative ways of increasing or decreasing, and by the end you can consider yourself an expert.

Line 'em up

Now that you are so clever and can knit pretty much anything, it's time to push on. Your next milestone will be to add a pattern, starting with some stripes. Simply add a new yarn at the beginning of a row in just the same way as when starting a new ball except that you don't cut off the old one. Work two, four or six rows so that you end up on the same side and switch back to the first yarn or add a different colour on either side. Great, isn't it?

Touchy feely

You really know you're making progress when you turn to textured knits. I think it's actually easier to work textured patterns than coloured ones, which is why I knitted an Aran sweater (which I still wear 20 years later) as one of my first projects. Lace patterns are also easier than they look, and make gorgeous summer tops and hats. All these designs are based around knit, purl, increase and decrease, although the pattern may introduce you to a new method of increase or decrease. The real trick is in keeping track of where you are in the pattern, and that's just a matter of experience. Soon it will become obvious what should be a purl and what should be a knit.

Socks appeal?

Socks are a love-it or hate-it thing. They will move you on to using double-pointed needles (if you haven't already used them on a hat) and will probably require you to use thinner-than-usual yarn, which shows how professional you are becoming. If you like to be different then there's nothing like wearing your own socks, but then again you may see no point in making items that spend 90% of the time hidden under your trousers. I have recently discovered the joys of sock knitting and I'm amazed how many ways you can do it. I particularly enjoy them because the tiny needles and single ball of yarn are so portable and because other people find it fascinating, especially once you reach the heel.

So darn fine

Even if you don't want to knit socks, I would advocate knitting with fine wool and small needles at some point because I want you to be a whole knitter who can do anything. You'll need this skill if you want to move on to Fair Isle, and if you wish you can try them both out at once. Alternatively, make yourself a skull cap or the like with a simple coloured pattern and smallish needles as a first stage.

Be fair

Fair Isle marks another step in the complexity of knitting. Fair Isle is the term now given to almost any type of coloured patterning, but true Fair Isle is knitted using two colours for each row, creating mostly geometrical patterns and generally using bright colours. Working successfully with two colours in a row is a question of correct tensioning. Everyone deals with this differently, and you'll need to find what works best for you. Elizabeth Zimmermann didn't believe it was necessary to constantly twist the two yarns together on the back, but said you shouldn't work a pattern that requires a yarn to travel behind more than five stitches. I take her advice partially. I work patterns that change colour over a greater distance than five stitches, but I twist the working yarn around my 'spare' yarn every four stitches or so, and that seems to work. Over short distances she is, of course, right, and there's no need to twist.

Picture this...

Intarsia is another challenge for the experienced knitter. This is the type of pattern where you have isolated motifs on a plain background, such as a bird or animal or something geometrical. Basically you are 'painting' a picture with your stitches. Separate yarns are used for each motif, so you could have quite a few ends to deal with. To prevent tangling, experts often wind sufficient yarn onto bobbins.

I've never tried this style of knitting because I have not yet seen a pattern that I like sufficiently, but there's no reason why you should have trouble with it.

Cutting edge

Cutting is a technique sometimes used for socks to insert an 'afterthought heel' or for sweaters and the like. It's not really difficult, but I put it near the end because of the courage it takes to do it. It's an idea best presented by Elizabeth Zimmermann, who discovered techniques to add anything from a pocket to a sleeve by cutting the knitting in the appropriate place, picking up the nearby stitches and then knitting on or attaching the new section.

Run wild!

If you have tried all of the above, or even if you haven't, you may be ready for the ultimate stage in the knitting journey: designing your own patterns. I've only recently started doing this; I began by working my own colour pattern in place of the pattern provided for the bag I was knitting. Changing the colours, patterns or yarns for a particular design like this is the easy way to design your own and it's a lot of fun. Designing from scratch is only a small step beyond this. Once you have knitted a test gauge in your yarn, it's just a question of working out how many rows and stitches you need to get the size you want.

> *All it takes to produce something beautiful is desire and experience.*
> *Vladimir Teriokhin*

True yarns

Knitting can be a thoroughly sociable craft. Somehow people relax when talking about their knits, barriers are lowered and we get to know the real them. Here are a few real-life stories from people who knit, showing that there are lots of ways to learn and many aspects to take your fancy. Everyone approaches knitting in an individual way and you can take it as far as you like. However you go about it, you'll find there's plenty of laughter to be had and friendships to be built along the way.

If at first you don't succeed...

If you learn anything from these true-life stories, it's that knitting projects don't always run smoothly. But as a knitter you have to learn to laugh about your mistakes, like Michael (see pages 44–45), and then move on. Take things slowly at first and read your pattern carefully. You may be lucky, like Jason (see pages 40–41), and sail through the process or you may struggle at first. Either way, you'll be a top knitter in the end if you persevere.

Salima's yarn...

Salima was first shown how to knit at school, but there was no one around to show her the ropes properly. 'I thought one day I'd find a nice granny to teach me, but when I was 20 I got bored of waiting for the ideal candidate and I bought a book that taught me how to knit. Then I got a book of Rowan patterns, chose an easy one and made that. From then on I never looked back.'

Knitting hasn't always run smoothly for Salima, but she knows how to turn mistakes to her advantage. 'One time I was knitting a polo neck onto a sweater in a lovely floaty yarn, but I was in a bit of a rush and instead of picking up stitches from around the neck I picked up stitches along one shoulder seam too. I only realized this when I came to join the shoulder seam. I had to unpick the neck but I didn't want to throw away all my hard work, so I removed the neck section and turned it into a scarf for my cat (above)!

'I've also sometimes overdone the knitting. One time I wanted to knit a very complicated cable pattern. I soon got bored and set it aside for ages. Then my parents asked me to cat sit while they went on holiday and I thought it was the perfect

opportunity to finish that cable knit. I went like the clappers to get it done, but then I noticed that my fingers were aching. I thought it was premature arthritis in that dramatic Indian 'Bollywood sensibility' way. So I took myself off to the doctor who told me I had repetitive strain injury. He asked me if I had been doing anything unusually straining with my hands and I couldn't think of anything at first. Then it dawned on me it was excessive amounts of cabling because I had been knitting for six hours a day for a week. I asked if that could be the

> **I thought it was premature arthritis in that dramatic Indian 'Bollywood sensibility' way**

reason. He laughed and said that he usually had to tell people of my age to drink and smoke and party less, but his advice to me was to knit less and get out more!'

Sitting pretty?
Even if it seems impossible to tear yourself away, take frequent breaks from your knitting to avoid strain and a potentially blush-inducing trip to the doctor.

Kerrie's yarn...

Kerrie's grandmother taught her to knit when she was around seven years old, but as is often the case, the novelty wore off after a while and she didn't knit anything for years. 'I was 19 when for some reason I decided that it would be fun to knit as many Mr Men as possible for my godson's second birthday. In my usual way I decided that I didn't need a pattern and armed myself with a bag of cheap acrylic yarn and a book containing pictures of all the Mr Men. A few months, 20 Mr Men and a happy two-year-old later I was done.'

It wasn't until she was pregnant with her first child that Kerrie seriously picked up her needles again and 'discovered the joys of pink fluffy novelty yarn'. She knitted away in her own little corner of the world, making Easter bunny slippers, hats and scarves, quite contented with her acrylic yarns and metal needles. But then, quite by accident, she came across knitting blogs. It was the start of something big. 'Suddenly I found a world where other people knitted, and used beautiful yarn I had never seen before. My eyes were opened to a new knitting arena, and it was at this point that my obsession exploded. Suddenly every corner of the house was filled with yarn – under the bed, in the wardrobe, in the chest of drawers. I set up my own blog,

www.kerriesplace.co.uk, and found myself making trips to unknown places to meet friends I had made online. My family and friends thought I was crazy, but I loved it. I knitted everywhere – on the train, in front of the TV, while cooking dinner – everywhere.'

Then one day Kerrie decided that she wanted more. She loved the online knitting world and craved to be an even bigger part of it, so she decided to set up her own online knitting magazine, www.magknits.com, which produced its first issue of free knitting patterns in February 2004. It went well, but 'as good as it was, it still wasn't enough'. Kerrie's patterns soon appeared in magazines and books.

> *I found a world where other people knitted, and used beautiful yarn I had never seen before.*

Blog on

A blog is short for weblog and is an online journal, which can be about all manner of things. Knitting blogs often include WIPs (works in progress) and comments about particular yarns or projects. The site's owner regularly posts the latest details of his or her personal knitting experiences and many sites have space for visitors to leave comments. You can start your own knitting blog free at www.blogger.com.

Meanwhile, she was also learning to sew and spin, resulting in another online magazine: *www.sewpretty.magknits.com*. Her novelty handspun yarns were sold in stores around the world. Still, this wasn't enough for Kerrie, and in August 2005 she bought *www.hipknits.co.uk* selling luxurious hand-painted yarns in natural fibres. Somehow Kerrie now manages to run all these sites as well as looking after her two children and holding down a full-time job in the IT industry. She still has a photo of those Mr Men on her noticeboard and rarely has fewer than four or five projects on her needles at any one time. She says: 'I firmly believe that you can do anything if you put your mind to it. You just need determination, a positive attitude and a little bit of luck.'

From simple knit 'n' purl…
Kerrie turned her passion for all things yarn into a series of successful businesses and never looked back. This is how many ventures begin – combining talent and enthusiasm to reach a larger audience, so why not knitting! Whether you just want to sell a few garments, start your own blog, or become a knitwear designer, there are plenty of ideas, as well as inspiration and information out there to get you started.

"Suddenly every corner of the house was filled with yarn – under the bed, in the wardrobe, in the chest of drawers…"

Jason's yarn...

One of a growing number of young male knitters, Jason is now passing on his skills to his wife and his daughter.

'I went to college in 1999 at a large public school in Illinois (Midwestern US) and while there I met the woman who is now my wife. From the moment we met in the first week of our freshman year, to this day, we have been inseparable. During our third year at college we decided we would quit smoking together. She figured it would be easier if she had something to keep her hands busy and to my surprise, she purchased a book on various needle arts including crochet, needlepoint, cross-stitch and knitting.

'At first I was surprised that she would be so interested in something that seemed fit for housewives and grandmothers, but I would glance through the book every once in a while and decided I would try it out. She picked up on crochet rather quickly – I tried to figure out knitting so I could help her. I also figured that it would keep my hands busy.

"Knitting has transformed in my mind into something that is more than just craft"

I picked up the book, a pair of needles, and some yarn and I was off. It seemed so easy to me. I was able to cast on following the pictures in the book, and the small practice rectangles I was making seemed to match up pretty well with the book's examples.

'Now, four years later, I've given knitted gifts to family members and friends, made things for my wife and daughter, and amassed a modest yarn stash that my wife (having learned to knit again just recently) is starting to raid.

> **My local yarn shop is run by people who don't care if a guy comes in to fondle the yarn.**

'As a 25-year-old man, it's hard sometimes to be a knitter. I'm lucky enough that my local yarn shop is run by people who don't care if a guy comes in to fondle the yarn. I've read plenty of stories by men who knit about being shooed out or receiving cold stares from store owners. My knitting habit is something that I've always kept to myself. I rarely knit in front of anyone other than my wife or daughter, although I've worked on projects while sitting at the yarn shop and people treat me with the same kindness that they treat everyone with.

'I think that there are a lot of stereotypes about men doing fibre arts. I really have a hard time with it, because I am a target of them and I don't agree with them. I've found a great online community of male knitters, and it has lifted my spirits to see them write about their work. Many of the male knitters

whose blogs I read are homosexual, and I think that's certainly a popular stereotype that people would have about male knitters. Obviously we're not all gay. The world seems to view knitting as such a feminine craft, possibly the ultimate feminine craft. Why is that? Men don't usually admit to knowing how to sew, but we respect tailors who do fine work. Most famous chefs are male but knitting is somehow so ultra-feminine that any man who tries it must be homosexual or just really strange.

'So many news articles and interviews have been published about men knitting that just focus on the "Wow, what's it like to be a man who knits?" that they never get down to the questions that they would ask any average knitter.

'I don't mean to diminish those authors or interviewees because maybe it's the way to slowly change the world. Once everyone gets over the astonishment of seeing a guy knitting, maybe it will become more accepted. I hope it does, because I know I plan to keep on knitting.'

Oh man!

Most women know someone who has met with discrimination simply because they are a woman in a man's world, but the reverse effect is obviously at work when it comes to knitting. If you are a man, take heart in the knowledge that you are not alone and seek out moral support on sites such as menknit. net. *As more and more of you take up knitting or come out of the closet it will become easier. And who knows, it may not be long before it's you who's saying 'Not tonight, darling'...*

Roberta's yarn...

Some people become obsessed with knitting as soon as they start, but for others, like Roberta, the fire smoulders for a while first.

'Knitting has crept quietly and unannounced into my life three times now, and it is only during the latest love affair that I have come to realize how deeply and subtly rewarding the relationship is. Two sticks and a ball of yarn; how can those mundane objects carry so much significance? Surely they are for granny types, clicking away at candyfloss-coloured baby booties. That's certainly my first memory of it – my mother knitting baby clothes for the local church bazaar. Along the way she taught me, and I started out knitting dolls' clothes because they were easy to complete. Later, when I was supposed to be revising for school exams, I would knit while watching TV because I could assuage the guilt of taking a break from my study with a double activity.

'My second encounter was more than a decade later, when I found that my baby son was only happy if he was sitting on my lap in the evening. I could only cope with so much television or music and I needed to feel more occupied. Knitting came to my rescue and I discovered a fascination for Fair Isle. I adore colour, and the possible combinations of Fair Isle patterns are endless. I knitted complex patterns on a small scale for my son and for friends' children to keep my brain active as well as my hands. I must have looked peculiar because I would integrate the spare colour of each row into the back of the knitting using my teeth to hold the yarn at the right tension. The knitting gave me so much pleasure that I continued

> *Two sticks and a ball of yarn; how can those mundane objects carry so much significance?*

Never felt like this before...

Felting, or fulling, is easy – sometimes too easy if that wasn't what you set out to do. You must use pure wool to achieve the dense, felt-like result. Just knit up your item far too large and machine-wash it on a cycle that's far too hot and far too rough. Basically you do everything wrong, and you do it deliberately – perfect for your inner bad girl!

with it long after my son's bedtime habits had sorted themselves out.

'Somewhere along the line I stopped knitting until I'd had my second and third children and found myself with a baby and toddler. I gave up work, and although I enjoy being with my children, I find that supervising play can be mindnumbingly dull. Reading or any other occupation that takes my eyes off the children is rarely possible, but knitting is a miracle. It can be picked up and dropped almost instantly. I can knit, watch and talk all at the same time, and if something requires action I can put my knitting aside and leap up. Any knitting feels useful, even if it is only a few rows.

'Now I have started to explore the magic of transforming knitting into felt. The shrinking and shaping is always unpredictable but it is extraordinary to knit something loose and floppy and apparently formless and have it emerge as a structure with substance and shape and in a completely different material. Colours and patterns are transformed too, so I can still play with Fair Isle and stripes to keep the knitting stimulating and enjoy how they smudge and blend when felted.'

Get fresh

Learning new techniques, flirting with colour, and taking the craft a step further are all ways of keeping your knitting new and exciting (like the start of any relationship). So every now and then, add a twist to your repertoire to keep the passion alive.

" **knitting** came to my **rescue** and I discovered a **fascination** for Fair Isle "

Michael's yarn...

For Michael, knitting was something that was thrust upon him. His friend Charles had wanted to learn for some time, but Michael was at first indifferent to the craft. 'Having just graduated from college, I believed I had a whole world to explore.' Six months after graduation, reality struck and so when Charles invited him over to dinner and a knitting lesson he went.

After dinner, Charles brought out two pairs of needles and his yarn and friend Dawn began the lesson. 'Dawn taught us the most unconventional style of knitting. After learning our slipknot, we then learned the "stab" cast on. Similar to the cast-on that knitters have used for hundreds of years, we draped the yarn over our hands and stabbed one needle through the space created by the yarn. We practised our knits and purls well into the night and I was surprised how satisfying it was.

'After a few weeks I had finished my first hat – a big rectangle sewn in half. It was in rainbow-coloured 100% acrylic yarn, and it was hideous and unfit to wear. In fact, over those first few months, I completed several hats, all either too large or too small. You see, despite her best intentions to show us the basics of knitting, Dawn had completely left out any discussion of gauge (the number of stitches per inch – better known as why garments fit the way they do). This, in turn, led to more than one expensive knitting disaster.

'Looking for interesting yarns, I bought two skeins of red and purple mohair/rayon bouclé yarn to make a basic triangular shawl. Still missing any hints on the topic of gauge, I pulled out my US 17 needles and knitted away. Then came the time to cast off. I remember seeing the words "CAST OFF LOOSELY" in big bold letters but I didn't care – I may have even said aloud, "Who are you? I'll cast off as tightly as I see fit – a shawl should cling to your shoulders!"

'I began to realize I had made a grave error. The bouclé prevented the edge from any give whatsoever. Frogging the edge proved to be ineffective. Frustrated, I took out my sharpest pair of scissors — "Well, if I can't rip it out, I'll just cut off the cast-off edge, pick up the stitches and do it again." I had taken a bad situation beyond the point of no return… I was approaching a Carrie level of irritation. Rather than burn my house to the ground, I calmly got up, grabbed a plastic grocery bag, put the shawl into the grocery bag, walked outside, and dropped it into the trash can.

> *I grabbed a plastic grocery bag, put the shawl into the grocery bag, walked outside, and dropped it into the trash can.*

'A few months later, I made my first gauge swatch. It's because of these first few experiences that my garments have good fit. And, luckily enough, not one has made it to the trash can since.'

Michael's first disasters haven't hindered his knitting career. He has now been knitting for just over five years and is co-founder of *menknit.net* and editor of the *menknit.net* e-zine. He teaches and designs from his studio in Washington, D.C.

> ## After a few weeks I had finished my first hat... in rainbow acrylic yarn, and it was hideous and unfit to wear!

Stay chilled

Knitting is a fascinating blend of technique and creativity, and is a guaranteed recipe for disaster at some point – for everyone! So don't get fraught when things go wrong – just take a deep breath and retrace your steps. If things do reach the point of no return (frogging or no frogging), just put it aside, and move onward and upward to the next wonderful project. A knit chick should never lose her cool – just accept that that particular project was not meant to be.

Men and tights

Knitting may be predominantly a female occupation at present, but once upon a time it was men's work. Indeed it is thought that the craft was spread to the West by Arabian sailors (men). Of course, the male knitters of the past set up guilds, or unions, and the first knitter's guild was established in Paris in 1527. Most of the knitters of the time made stockings, or in fact items that were effectively tights, with underpants and stockings all in one. So although women had to wait until the 1960s for tights, men had really invented them more than 400 years earlier.

What's your style?

Are you a dedicated knitter or just interested in enhancing your image by taking up a trendy hobby? Do you knit for pleasure, productivity or show? Try this light-hearted quiz to find out what motivates you.

1 As a finalist on *Who Wants to be a Millionaire* your crucial question is 'Where does the finest sheep's wool come from?'

Do you answer:

A The Merino sheep
B Australia
C *www.billysbarnstore.com*

2 Repetitive strain injury in your hands is a result of:

A Voraciously knitting complicated patterns.
B Knitting too tightly and tensely.
C Losing the key for the handcuffs and trying to wriggle them off.

3 You inherit an enormous four-poster bed from a relative. Do you:

A Knit an equally impressive bedspread to go on it.
B Buy a nice duvet and knit a teddy bear or a couple of furry cushion covers.
C Stay in bed all weekend.

4 You decide to knit something for the thing you love most in life. Is it:

A A jumper for your partner.
B A coat for your dog or cat.
C A cover for your MP3 player.

5 You are unable to take your knitting needles on a long haul flight because they are considered a security risk. Do you:

A Take a boat instead.
B Take some chopsticks with you and do what you can with these.
C Take the pilot.

6 A former friend offers you one of his Merino sheep to keep your grass down. Do you:

A Accept gleefully and take a course on shearing.

B Say yes and then settle for a sheepskin rug and buy lots of mint sauce.

C Decline but take up shearing anyway because of the Aussie hunk/babe running the course.

7 **Your partner suggests a holiday in Alaska. Is this:**

A Music to your ears. You start knitting straight away.

B Alarming – you invest in thermal underwear and a hot-water bottle, but you do knit a nice cover for the hottie.

C A good excuse to move to Spain with your partner's best friend.

8 **Aunt Muriel is coming for Christmas. She always gives you one of her knitted tea cosies. Do you give her:**

A A hand-knitted cover for her Zimmer frame.

B Some nicer knitting patterns.

C A copy of this book.

9 **Your partner's birthday looms and you feel something special is in order. Do you:**

A Knit a chunky jumper to keep him warm when you go away.

B Knit a scarf and buy a bottle of finest malt whisky.

C Knit yourself a thong and give him his present along with a shared bottle of champagne.

10 **You are interviewed for local radio. The first question is 'What is so good about knitting?' Do you reply:**

A For 30 minutes solid, hardly taking breath between sentences.

B That it is a creative and relaxing way to put up with public transport.

C That knits feel so sexy when you don't wear anything else underneath.

Answers

Mostly As You are clearly a dedicated and highly devoted knitter. In fact you would do well sharing your talents. Why not offer to show kids how to knit at your local school, set up a club knitting items for a good cause or start your own knit blog?

Mostly Bs You are a highly competent knitter and getting better all the time. Knitting doesn't rule your life, though – not yet.

Mostly Cs Knitting is like a stylish accessory for you. You knit for fun, enjoy the social side of it and don't let it stand in your way.

Shop till you drop

Fanciable fibres

Yarns can be made from just about anything furry or fibrous – if you thought the choice was simply between lambswool and acrylic, you're missing out. There's never been a better time to be a knitter because there's never been such an exciting and sumptuous array of yarns around, and the choice is growing all the time. New yarns are being developed all the time; you can even find yarns made from apparently unlikely materials such as bamboo. Here's a quick run-through of the tempting types of yarn that are available at the moment.

Sheep's wool

This is a brilliant all-rounder that comes in lots of varieties – just like sheep. Whatever your choice, you can be sure wool will be warm in winter, cool in summer, fairly wind- and waterproof and snug even when wet. Choose according to taste: yarn from Icelandic sheep (Lopi yarn) can be coarse but it's very strong and durable; Shetland wool is a good medium type of wool; and merino is the softest, most lovely and least itchy, although it does tend to pill.

> *Soft wool from the simple silly sheep can be as fine as a cobweb, tough and strong as string, as light and soft as down.*
>
> Elizabeth Zimmermann
> (Knitting Without Tears)

Alpaca

The number-one choice if excessive warmth and softness
are a priority comes from the coat of an alpaca, which looks
likes its close relative the llama, and originates in South
America. Even today, nearly all alpaca comes from Peru,
though the US is beginning to build up its own herds. Alpaca
is dense, warm and unlikely to pill. It is a good choice for
warm, hard-wearing items such as blankets, hats and gloves,
but a sweater might live up to its name unless worn in very
cold conditions.

Mohair

Popular in the 1960s, this is a
very soft, fluffy yarn from the
coat of the angora goat. It's
light and warm and sheds
dirt well, but it can be
itchy and is so soft that
it is often blended with
a bit of acrylic to hold
it together. It is both
flame-resistant and
sound-absorbent.

Cashmere

Another yarn from our friend the goat. With cashmere, the wool is combed only from the belly of the animal, producing a super-soft but expensive yarn. It's very warm and ideal for a luxury item, but it is so soft that it can wear away, so a blend with wool is a good idea. If you are putting a lot of work into, say, an Icelandic-style sweater, you may wish to match your effort with this type of yarn to produce a superlative item.

Angora

Another super-soft, fluffy yarn that's lovely to touch but can shed rather badly and can cause sneezing. For that reason it is often blended, especially with pure wool or silk, which makes a great soft but strong yarn. It is also sometimes blended with wool because angora alone has no elasticity, making it harder to knit with than wool. The fibre comes from the fur of the angora rabbit, and is combed from the animal every few days.

Silk

Spun from the cocoons of the silk worm, it's best not to think about how the poor little worms were plunged into boiling water to extract the stuff because this is such a lovely yarn. It's lustrous, smooth, lightweight and cool, not to mention incredibly strong, making it ideal for a host of uses, especially for summer or eveningwear items.

Linen

This yarn comes from the flax plant. It's stronger than cotton, very smooth and cool to wear, but not very flexible or stretchy. It makes a luxurious summer top or works well in blends for other items. Like cotton, it doesn't cause allergies.

Bamboo

This yarn has a lovely sheen, and is cool to the touch, like cotton or linen. It is also said to knit up nicely. Bamboo, the fastest-growing plant on the planet, has many other uses: for scaffolding, buildings and furniture; to make paper, mats, flooring and musical instruments; and even as food – the young shoots and the grain can be eaten.

Soy

This is another wonder product of nature. The yarn made from the waste product of the tofu industry is said to be as soft as cashmere, as pliable as wool and as smooth as silk. Many knitters who have used it rave about its easy-knit qualities.

Cotton

Cotton is spun from the fibre surrounding the seeds of the cotton plant. It is light and cool to wear, but not as easy to knit with as wool because it lacks stretch. For this reason, some manufacturers blend it with wool to create a more versatile yarn. Cotton doesn't cause any allergies.

Rayon

This is made from wood pulp and includes a number of products under its umbrella, including viscose. The yarn is cool to the touch, dyes well and is strong, with a distinct sheen, making it a good basis for some of the modern novelty yarns. It knits well and can be used alone or as part of a blend.

Acrylic

This synthetic material dyes in bright colours, washes well, is inexpensive and is a common ingredient of novelty yarns. If used alone it can be squeaky – wool blend generally works best, even for baby garments, where easy care is essential.

Nylon

Nylon is another versatile synthetic material. It is often favoured for use in baby clothes, and is a fibre that can work really well in a blend. Nylon's main attribute, apart from being easy to wash, is its strength – most sock yarns have a bit of nylon somewhere in their mix.

Polyester

Polyester is an easy-care yarn that is resistant to shrinkage, and is quick-drying and durable, but as you will know if you have polyester sheets, it can be hot and sticky unless used in a blend.

Shoppers' paradise

Thanks to the Internet, we are no longer confined to our own neighbourhood for shopping, and it is now easy to buy yarns and other goodies from all over the world. Try out some of the following options – you may get a better bargain than you thought, or find a better service, which is worth its weight in gold.

Going local

A yarn store is an absolute Aladdin's cave for knitters – it's most likely you've spent many hours in one of these just gazing at the colours and textures. It's a fabulous opportunity to feel the yarns for yourself and have a good rummage. This can be a great place to meet other knitters and obtain advice on the latest yarns, equipment and bargains that knitters adore. Don't be stingy and choose what you want in the shop only to buy it cheaper over the Internet. If everybody does this then there soon won't be any yarn shops around and there'll be no popping out for a pair of needles; you'll have to pay the postage and wait for the package to arrive.

A yarn store is an absolute Aladdin's cave for knitters

Spinning around

Using the Internet or a mail-order service, it is often possible to buy yarn from the spinner, which could save you money and is often more satisfying than going through a retailer. Some of these suppliers are organic or use special dyeing methods, which is always interesting to hear about and adds character to your knits. You'll find advertisements from some of the smaller suppliers in knitting magazines, or you may be lucky enough to get a recommendation. You might even find a local spinner near you, in which case you may be able to visit their shop and find an even better bargain in the end-of-line section.

Wool from the web

If you don't know what to buy and haven't got a reasonably large yarn shop near you, then check out some of the larger yarn suppliers such as *kaleidoscopeyarns.com* or *yarn-shop.co.uk*. These supply many of the leading brands as well as a good range of needles, patterns and accessories.

Holiday romances

If you have fallen in love with a foreign yarn, check out the price in the country of origin, as it can be much cheaper there. The British, for example, tend to think that everything costs less abroad, particularly in the US. However, British yarns, such as those produced by Rowan and Jaeger, are actually cheaper in the UK than in the US. For this reason, it is worthwhile for knitters in the US to buy British-sourced yarns from the UK and pay for the postage.

RIGHT: There's nothing like going to your local yarn store to see and touch the yarns on offer.

Fair's fair

Craft fairs have always been a good place to find a bargain, to see the newest items that have come onto the market, and be inspired by fresh ideas. You can often pick up lessons and advice too, and talk to knitters, spinners and designers. If you live in the US, check out the venues organized by the Yarn Council of America and look up events at *knittersreview.com*; if you live in the UK, check out *bhkc.co.uk*, part of *ukhandknitting.com*.

Bargain bay

If you want only a small amount of yarn, you might find a bargain from eBay, if someone is auctioning off their leftovers. For larger amounts, look at the eBay store sites – you can often find inexpensive end-of-line batches. Don't get caught up in a buying frenzy, though. If an item is being auctioned, decide what your limit is by comparing prices elsewhere and stick to it; otherwise you could end up paying more than you would from a shop.

Shoppers' know-how

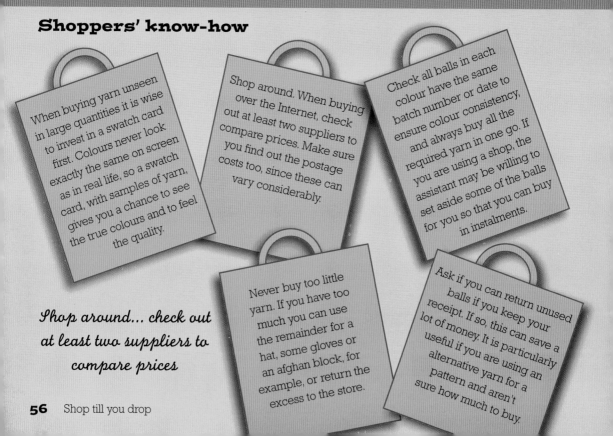

When buying yarn unseen in large quantities it is wise to invest in a swatch card first. Colours never look exactly the same on screen as in real life, so a swatch card, with samples of yarn, gives you a chance to see the true colours and to feel the quality.

Shop around. When buying over the Internet, check out at least two suppliers to compare prices. Make sure you find out the postage costs too, since these can vary considerably.

Check all balls in each colour have the same batch number or date to ensure colour consistency, and always buy all the required yarn in one go. If you are using a shop, the assistant may be willing to set aside some of the balls for you so that you can buy in instalments.

Never buy too little yarn. If you have too much you can use the remainder for a hat, some gloves or an afghan block, for example, or return the excess to the store.

Ask if you can return unused balls if you keep your receipt. If so, this can save a lot of money. It is particularly useful if you are using an alternative yarn for a pattern and aren't sure how much to buy.

Shop around... check out at least two suppliers to compare prices

"Whoever said **money** can't buy happiness **simply** didn't **know** where to go **shopping**"

Bo Derek

Choices, choices

I once saw a short silent film in which a small, seemingly innocuous, elderly lady visits a series of fruit shops, squeezing the fruit more and more violently each time until she is finally chased out by an outraged assistant. Every time I visit a yarn store, the image of the little old lady comes into my head as I furtively squeeze the balls. Like her, I just can't help myself, and once I start it is impossible to stop. So my question to you is, how do you choose your yarn?

The pattern

Most decision-making about a yarn is based on the desirability of the pattern that goes with it. This is because the majority of knitters choose a pattern and then make it in the named wool, taking control only of the colour choice. As your confidence increases, or if you have a knitting guru on hand, you should consider using an alternative wool in the same weight instead. Your local yarn shop may be able to supply advice on suitable options. Meanwhile, the Yarn Council of America is trying to get yarn sizes standardized using a number system, which will make substitutions much easier.

Yarn snobs like me can tell how many synthetics are in a mix

The looks

First impressions count. Just as most people decide whether or not to buy a house within the first three minutes of seeing it, a knitter falls for a yarn on sight. Only if it drastically fails the following touch tests will she change her mind, and even then, she may try to find an alternative use for it.

The manufacturer

The packaging on the yarn – that thin band of paper – and the reputation of the manufacturer have a major effect on the desirability of a yarn. Sometimes we want to buy a particular wool just because we like the clean lines of the design on the wrapper or any images it includes. Other times we might pick out a yarn because we've already bought another one by the same manufacturer and we love it or because everyone says that the company makes the best yarns.

The yarn content

As you saw from pages 50–53, how a yarn turns out largely depends on the fibres it contains. The label won't tell us the quality of those fibres, but by identifying the types we will get a good idea of what to expect. Yarn snobs like me can tell how many synthetics are in the mix.

RIGHT: Yarn has tremendous sensory appeal – we're drawn to touch and feel it, and revel in the array of colours available.

"*Stick your face right into that ball and breathe in. I've no idea what purpose this serves, but I always find myself doing it anyway!*"

The cost

It's not always how cheap a yarn is that counts, but sometimes how expensive it is. The old adage 'you get what you pay for' comes to mind and the temptation can be to buy the best you can afford. Watch out for this one. Although major brands do often provide high quality, you sometimes pay just for a name and may be able to find a similar or better quality for less. Likewise, just because a yarn is discounted by 50% doesn't mean you should buy it unless you like it.

The squeeze

Take the ball of yarn in your hand, squeeze it and relax. The amount the ball compresses in your hand and the speed at which it recovers its shape tells you about the yarn's loft – how soft and springy it is. A yarn with a lot of loft is likely to be warm. Mohair yarns, for example, have a high loft.

The skin test

Lightly pass the ball over your arm or cheek in a caress. This tells you how itchy the yarn is. If you are making a bag or jacket this isn't all that important, but if you are making a top or a tight-fitting sweater you need to be sure it won't have you scratching and jigging about. If you know that you have sensitive skin, hold the ball to your skin for a minute or so to see if any reaction develops. Alternatively, limit your purchases to synthetics and yarns made from plant fibres, which are unlikely to cause a problem.

The inhale

Stick your face right into that ball and breathe in. I've no idea what purpose this serves, but I always find myself doing it anyway. I like to do it as a follow-up to the skin test, passing the ball over my cheek to my nose and pausing to inhale. Actually, I do think that smell is important. I prefer natural yarns, and by sniffing it I can see if there is any kind of synthetic, chemical smell.

The finger roll

Always a good one, this involves rubbing a length of the yarn between finger and thumb. It tells you several things about the yarn: its thickness, density and strength. You won't need to do this with a standard worsted or double knitting wool, but some yarns, such as those containing a high quantity of cashmere or angora, may be very delicate, and this test will help you judge whether the yarn will be strong enough. It also helps you gauge how it will knit, by whether it slides easily through your fingers or handles less smoothly.

> " The only way to get rid of temptation is to yield to it. Resist it, and your soul grows sick with longing for the things it has forbidden itself. "
>
> Oscar Wilde (The Picture of Dorian Gray)

What's your type?

Yarns change as fast as catwalk fashions, so if you see a great yarn you need to get it and knit quickly because you'll soon spot another, equally delectable one. Trends change fast, but it is possible to show examples of the types of yarns around to help you decide what you yearn for and what you wouldn't have if it were given away free.

Slinkily slender

I'd almost be tempted to skip over fine yarns because we aren't interested in taking a lifetime to make one item here. However, the fact is that this group of yarns combines brilliantly with chunkier yarns to create unique textures, and if you want your knits to stand out from the crowd then incorporating one of these could be the answer. They're also great if you are interesting in doing something artistic with the basic fabric of your knits because it enables you, in effect, to make your own yarn. Any of them could be combined with thicker yarns to create something truly gorgeous. Run two or more yarns together; use an extra yarn to create a stripe or border; or buy a selection pack of fine yarns and work stripes into your knits at random. In fact, I can feel my fingers itching to knit already. Just run your main yarn and the fine yarn through your fingers together and knit as one. It is really that simple. Don't fuss too much about how the yarns lie: sometimes one yarn will lie at the front, sometimes the other one will; that random patterning is all part of the appeal – it's knitting into the unknown.

Minxy middles

The majority of yarns around today fall into the worsted or double knitting range. They are of medium thickness and perfect for making your average cardigan, jumper, hat or gloves. Don't be put off by the word 'average', because when it comes to these yarns it's what you do with them that counts, not what they look like. Ordinary, medium-weight, plain or modestly patterned yarns are perfect when it comes to knitting texture into your garments with cables or rib variations. They also show off lacy patterns, scallops and other motifs to perfection, so this is the ideal type of yarn to use for intarsia patterns and stripes. You have a huge choice here when it comes to quality and texture, so feel your way around your local knitting shop, squeezing the yarns and caressing the angoras and you'll soon be won over. The medium-weight category is also a rich source of natural fibres. They don't tend to stretch or shed, flowing smoothly through your fingers – this makes for a most sensuous experience.

Feel your way around your local knitting shop, squeezing the yarns and caressing the angoras

To dye for
Hand-dyed yarns are so delicious that the
temptation is to buy first, think later. If you
can't afford them, release your creative
urges and dye your own yarn using fabric
dyes. Just mix up the colours, pour them
over the yarn as artistically as you like,
then follow the manufacturer's instructions.

Va va va voluptuous

Some of the most exciting yarns are highly textured or chunky, and use very big needles. These provide a satisfying quick knit – essential if you want to finish your knit while it's still catwalk-cool, and just the thing for the knit fashionistas amongst us. Very fibrous varieties, such as the eyelash or fake fur yarns and rag styles, will hide a multitude of knitting errors, so are great for beginners.

Textured and chunky yarns provide a satisfyingly quick knit

Bobble yarns and bouclés are great if you want to create something different but not *too* way out. They come in all sorts of textures and finishes, and you get a good idea of how they will knit up just by looking at the ball or hank. Some bouclés can be a little coarse, so pass the ball over your cheek before you buy to check the feel-factor.

Chenille has a wonderful, super-soft, velvety feel that produces knits with a gloriously lush texture, often in rich colours. I find this yarn slightly awkward to work with because its heavy pile means that it doesn't slide readily through your fingers and it can stretch a little or shed. Chenille is a great yarn to use for anything that will be in close contact with your skin, especially hats, scarves and sweaters.

Puppy love

Ever wondered what to do with all that dog hair that sticks to furniture? If you collect the hairs from your pet, you can get them spun into yarn. But be warned – you need 10oz (285gm) for a scarf alone. Dog yarn is officially called Chiengora, and is 80% warmer than sheep's wool. Check out the VIP Fibres website.

Fake fur yarns come in natural or truly wild colours. Most are easy-care and knit up like long-pile fur fabric, but you can buy pure wool versions for other finishes. The Jaeger version in kid mohair and wool knits up like a luxurious sheepskin rug. Use it for plush gilets, hats, scarves, cushions and throws.

Rag-style yarns give a lovely long-pile texture that's great to snuggle into

Eyelash yarn is very similar to the fake-fur varieties, but with no attempt to make it look like fur. It's just fluffy for the sheer fun of it.

Rag-style yarns have ragged pieces of cloth hanging off at regular intervals and knit up rather like a crazy rag rug. These are absolutely brilliant for jazzy bags and scarves and knit up surprisingly easily. You get a lovely long-pile texture that's great to snuggle into. Most of these yarns are soft and easy to wash and care for.

Sari silk is a fascinating novelty yarn. It is made from off-cuts of silk left over from sari manufacture, so no two skeins are the same. Sari silks are irresistible to the knitting daredevil, as the yarns are different every time. You may want to knit a small project such as a hat or scarf if you're trying it for the first time, or work stripes from different hanks across a larger item to produce an even spread of colours.

Sari silks are irresistible to the knitting daredevil as the yarns are different every time

The ethical knitter

There are many yarns around to please the ethical yarn consumer. Try sari silk yarn (from Hip Knits or the Fibre Craft Studio), which is mainly woven by refugees, or Manos del Uruguay (Kaleidoscope Yarns), which is spun by a women's cooperative in Uruguay. You can buy organic wool from ever-increasing sources – including one that is 'guaranteed predator friendly' because when eaten the organic sheep won't hurt the predator!

Thick and thin yarns are often handspun and, as the name suggests, vary in thickness from thick to thin. The yarn looks difficult to use, but actually you just knit away on fairly large needles and produce a knit with a lovely touchy-feely finish. Intriguingly, you can see through the knit where the yarn is thin, and not where it is thick, which always makes people look twice if you're feeling saucy. Depending on the yarn, you can use it for almost anything from a summer vest to a winter scarf or hat.

Tape yarns look difficult to use but produce a knit with a lovely touchy-feely finish

Tape yarns are basically ribbons. They are usually made of cotton or synthetics and produce a lovely fabric-like finish. Most require quite large needles, and they knit up fast and loose. They work well for summer tops, so you can still be knitted out when the temperature rises.

I've just gotta have it!

You know that you don't really need any more accessories for knitting apart from needles, but, like most things in life, there are many delectable items out there that give immense pleasure just to look at. A happy knitter is a good knitter, so maybe you do need them... Here are a few of the most tempting bits of kit to get your fingers twitching.

Get to the point

You're familiar with grey metal needles. They are commonly used and quite cheap, but are rather drab. So what's more appealing?

Bamboo needles These are smooth and lightweight, plus the colour of these needles is delightfully neutral so they match every shade of yarn – so chic! They have 'green' appeal too, because bamboo is a fast-growing, renewable natural material.

Casein This is a product of the dairy industry and completely natural. With their light-as-air feel, the needle's silky surface comes in fabulous finishes including tortoiseshell and brights. They're hard to get hold of – I treasure my jazzy red pair.

Wooden needles You can't go wrong, and the options are simply endless. If you're prepared to invest serious money on your needles, you can select from various exotic woods and ones that are finished with fantastic glass beads.

The colour of bamboo needles is delightfully neutral so they match every shade of yarn – so chic!

Antique needles Or should we call them 'vintage'? If you like digging around in junk stores or going to auctions and fairs, you might get lucky. These could be made out of unsavoury material such as ivory or tortoiseshell, but some people would pay a lot of money for them, so they could be a good investment for the financially clued-up knitters among us.

Hold that look

Who could resist a few cute additions to their kit?

Knitting bags Knitters on the go know that a great bag is essential. Whether they are made of leather or fabric, are totes or backpacks, we'll simply *never* have enough bags…

Needle roll Your make-up brushes have one, so why not your lovingly collected sticks? Design your own and store your needles in the luxury they deserve.

Row counter Ideal for the lazy knitter, or when you're glued to the TV – especially when fluffy yarns make it almost impossible to count the rows.

Stitch holder For holding knitted pieces that you can't yet bind off. Also essential for unfaithful knitters; you know – the ones who are easily seduced by a new pattern before finishing with the old one.

Stitch markers Needed for items where you have to increase or decrease at a set position on each round… although you might not care what they're for, when they look so lovely. You can buy gorgeous beaded markers in irresistible colours. Threaded onto looped wire, they also double up as earrings, pendants and bag charms. You might just use them for your knitting when you're in the mood.

Let's slip (knot) away

In 1966, a Russian spy escaped from London's Wormwood Scrubs prison in a James Bond-style escape using a homemade rope ladder to scale the 20ft wall – each rung was a knitting needle! So, take your needle roll everywhere – you never know when you might need to make a speedy getaway…

You're in good company

Taking back the knit

The image of knitting has been revolutionized in the last few years. Once associated with everything fusty, dowdy and frumpy, knitting has now been taken up by a new generation – young and old, men, women and kids – who knit for fun, for fashion, for creativity and for relaxation.

Out with the old

In *Stepford Wives*, Glenn Close plays Mrs Wellington, who is having a book discussion with the town's robotically perfect ladies. She announces that today's book says to her, 'Let's celebrate the birth of Our Lord Jesus Christ with yarn'. That about sums up what most of us thought knitting was about twenty years ago – aunty making tasteless Christmas decorations or foul items of clothing that we were supposed to admire. It was about wealthy housewives with time on their hands. But now there's been such a dramatic turnaround that if aunty suggests knitting something for Christmas we might actively encourage the idea. If aunty could be persuaded to make a cover for an MP3 player– and preferably provide the MP3 player to go inside – then yes please.

Actually, today it's not just the great aunts and grandmothers in our lives who knit, but also mums and sisters, and increasingly dads, uncles and brothers too. It is true that there is still a lingering idea that men who knit must be gay (see Jason's viewpoint on this, page 41) but this is gradually beginning to shift, especially as heterosexual film stars such as David Arquette are coming out of the closet and admitting that they knit (see page 74). And in the end, knitting isn't about our gender or sexual preferences or anything else of a personal nature. It's about constructing things, controlling the way they look and having a skill, and that's something ingrained in us all, even before we had our first Lego sets.

> *Knitting is about constructing things, controlling the way they look and having a skill*

Who's knitting now?

So if it's not just grannies and great aunts who are knitting now, just who are today's knitters? The Yarn Council of America carried out a survey in autumn 2004 and found that women aged 25–34 were increasingly keen on the craft. In fact, between 2002 and 2004 their share of the knitting market rose from 13% to an impressive 33%. But other groups were on the increase too. According to the survey, the number of knitters who were aged 18 years and under doubled in the same three-year period. What's more, these people are all avid knitters. Research showed that people who bought yarn in 2004 made an unbelievable 15.3 projects in that year. Some of the people out there must be doing a hell of a lot of knitting, because I don't come close to filling my quota for the year.

The really good news is that if you are in the under-35 category then the pattern designers and yarn manufacturers are after your business. As a member of the fastest-expanding group of knitters, you are the main target. This means that there will be plenty more patterns appearing to tickle your fancy as well as a new array of desirable yarns. Your opinions are also likely to be noted, so if you want something specific and can't manage to find it, try contacting the yarn manufacturers or pattern houses and telling them what's missing from the shelves – you might even be responsible for the creation of a new line of wool. And if you are a male knitter, you should speak out too. Your numbers are beginning to grow impressively and soon you will find more and more things coming on the market that are aimed specifically at you.

The knitterati

You probably won't be driven to take up knitting just because the rich and famous do it – although if Johnny Depp or Orlando Bloom suddenly announced that they found it sexy to watch a woman knit you might be justly tempted – but it is nice to know that you are in good company. Here are some names to inspire you. You may be surprised by some of them, but given that a third of all American and British women are at it, it shouldn't come as such a shock that film stars do it too.

Courtney Cox was so busy knitting on the set of *Friends* one time that apparently Monica (Courtney) and Phoebe (Lisa Kudrow) carried on going when the cameras started rolling. Married to another knitter, David Arquette, Courtney doesn't have to look far for a fellow to give her some friendly knitting advice or a second opinion on a pattern.

David Arquette has been photographed knitting, and not just for a publicity stunt. He really does knit, though he may not appreciate the paparazzi sticking their long lenses over the wall to catch him doing it.

Cameron Diaz is one of many film stars said to knit on set to keep boredom at bay, along with Gwyneth Paltrow and Sandra Bullock.

Madonna is said to find it as relaxing to knit a sweater as to have a session of yoga. Maybe that's where the suggestion that knitting is the new yoga came from.

Richard Gere is another top star who is said to knit on set, though I can hardly credit it.

Goldie Hawn is a regular knitter, and after the events of 9/11 she reached for her needles to knit the American flag. 'I think, in my own small way, I was trying to knit America back together,' she said. She isn't the only one to reach for the needles after 9/11. Apparently there was a nationwide, if not international, move towards traditional crafts in the wake of the event as people sought calm and reassurance through the creative process of crafting.

Daryl Hannah likes to knit, though she admits that she's no expert and claims that 'I don't even know how to purl'. However, in *Vogue Knitting* magazine (Fall 2003) she talks like a devotee, saying 'I usually have an idea or theme in my head to start with. I fall in love with the colours and textures of yarns.' She jokes that 'I only make scarves. I did make a hat once, but even that started out as a scarf.' Like Julia Roberts, she likes to knit on a film set because it's calming and doesn't require total concentration.

Martha Stewart famously emerged from federal prison in March 2005 wearing a poncho made by a friend inside. Such is Martha's status in the US that everyone wanted one, and the Craft Yarn Council of America was flooded with requests for the pattern. Several versions emerged – if you want to knit your own, you can find free patterns at the Craft Yarn Council site and elsewhere on the net.

Knitting ban

Star knitters beware – directors may not think you are taking your work seriously if you knit too much on set. In 2003, teachers in northern India were banned from knitting in classrooms because the authorities believed they weren't giving their full attention to pupils. According to the Principal Secretary of Education in the region 'there were complaints that often teachers would do their personal knitting during school hours'. Kaffe Fassett came down on the side of the teachers, pointing out that 'people concentrate better when they knit'. So get clicking between takes!

Eartha Kitt made a fabulous scarf for *Celebrity Scarves* (see page 78) along with Daryl Hannah, Rikki Lake, Courtney Thorne Smith and others. The book raises money for the American Foundation for AIDS Research.

Catherine Zeta Jones is one of the major league star knitters, along with Julia Roberts, who has helped to transform knitting from geek to chic. Apparently, she knitted an impressive 15 ponchos and helped start a bit of a craze. The rest, as they say, is history.

Russell Crowe is said to knit. There's a great picture of him knitting that has led excited knitters everywhere to believe that he not only enjoys the craft but is also actually quite good at it. Sadly, the truth is that he simply grabbed some nearby knitting for the shot as a laugh. However, do give me a ring, Russell, if I'm wrong, and I'll gladly set the record straight.

Geri Halliwell was snapped knitting between takes during the filming of an episode of *Sex and the City* – and it wasn't just a simple hat or scarf she was making either, but a rather nice sweater.

Mary-Louise Parker knitted a hat for her actor boyfriend Billy Crudup. She gave up smoking and took up knitting because, as she says, 'you can't do both at once. I can't, anyway'. She adds: 'So kids, put down that tobacco and pick up some needles. Wait, that doesn't sound right...'

Eva Herzigova, proves that models do it too. She has knitted since she was a teenager, it seems. British model Stella Tennant also likes to wield the pins.

Saintly celebs

Knit up your favourite star's pattern from *Celebrity Scarves* (Sixth & Spring Books) and know that in the process you're giving money to charity. How heavenly – you're entitled to a smug smile as you click.

Other knitters with the knack:

Madeleine Albright
Lynne Cheney
Rosie Grier
Rose McGowan
Julianne Moore
Kate Moss
Sarah Jessica Parker
Winona Ryder
Brooke Shields
Joanne Woodward

Uma Thurman was spotted in Suss Design in Los Angeles buying yarn, knitting needles and a T-shirt emblazoned with a picture of a woman knitting in the nude. She was also seen in a yarn shop in New York buying yet more needles and yarn, showing that if you are famous you can't buy anything without everybody knowing exactly what is in the bag – the yarn from Suss Design was cashmerino, by the way, and Uma bought 26 balls. So keen is Uma on knitting that she is even said to have asked an assistant in a Santa Monica craft store if her four-year-old daughter was too young to learn – good on her.

Hilary Swank, Oscar-winning star of *Million Dollar Baby*, professes to enjoy this hobby – along with sky diving, river rafting and skiing (need I say more).

Julia Roberts has been knitting for years and has even devised her own striped pullover pattern, which appeared in *McCalls Magazine* (January 2001). Indeed she once mused that her dream was to run her own knitting shop. She is happy to talk about her favourite hobby and on the *Oprah* show she revealed that it was a man who had first taught her – a painter on the set of *The Pelican Brief*. She enjoys knitting with friends and finds it passes the time nicely on set: 'I can sit on a set between shots, chat with people and just knit away'. Indeed, while on the set of *Mona Lisa Smile* she is said to have taught co-stars Julia Stiles, Maggie Gyllenhaal and Kirsten Dunst how to knit. She even wore one of her own knitted hats in *Stepmom*.

Knit
parade

Knitting inspirations

Fun and exciting knitting patterns are everywhere, but where do the designers get their ideas, and can you get unique designs by following their lead? Designers get inspired by designs from abroad, from the past and from the catwalk, and yes, you can do the same thing. If you want to do your own trendsetting, look out for vintage patterns, and knit one up in today's colours – you could become quite a style guru. The following pages show samples of the knitwear looks of past decades, some embarrassingly awful but others really quite knittable.

Looking first at inspirational knitting influences from abroad, you will find that the Andean style (found in Peru, Argentina, Chile and Bolivia, for example) has a steady appeal, with its intricate patterning and attractive figurative motifs, illustrating stylized birds, flowers and animals. This is a style that is not so very different from the beautifully complex Fair Isle patterns that have been popular in the West since the 1930s.

Andean style has a steady appeal, with its intricate patterning and attractive figurative motifs

A totally different look that originated off the shores of Britain in traditional fishing communities is that of the chunky Arans and Guernseys, with their ornate textural designs. These have come back into fashion again and again over the years, but notably in the 1970s with the *Starsky and Hutch* look.

Some designers are influenced by designs in other mediums. For example, you can see something of the American patchwork quilting and European tapestry in the work of renowned knitwear designers such as Debbie Bliss and Kaffe Fassett.

Other knitwear designers draw on the textiles of African and Asian traditions, for example, helping to enrich Western designs with the colours and images of other cultures. Crossing the boundaries of one medium to another is an excellent way of bringing a new twist to a design while still having references to draw on.

> *There's never a new fashion but it's old!*
> Geoffrey Chaucer (The Canterbury Tales)

RIGHT: Knitwear designers seek inspiration from knitting traditions around the world.

The shapely '30s

The 1930s was a decade when women were women, and Joan Crawford, Mae West, Lana Turner and Jean Harlow were the leading ladies of the day. Gone was the boyish flapper look of the 1920s. Instead, ladies' fashions celebrated a more voluptuous figure, held in shape by corsets or bras with girdles. Clothing was close-fitting and skirt lengths dropped to the ankle or mid-calf to give a slim and elegant silhouette. Fine knitwear showed off shapely curves, and Lana Turner's rise to fame owed much to a figure-hugging baby-blue cashmere sweater. She was one of the first 'sweater girls', who were popular as pin-ups.

The big crash

While Hollywood was projecting a glamorous, elegant image, life was hard in the real world. Nearly every family felt the repercussions of the Wall Street Crash of October 24 1926 and the long Depression that followed. Gone was the reckless partying and shopping of the early 1920s. For most people garments could be replaced only when absolutely necessary, and many girls turned to sewing and knitting as an affordable way to produce something new and stylish.

> *I like my clothes to be tight enough to show I'm a woman... but loose enough to show I'm a lady.*
>
> Mae West

Enduringly simple

In England in 1936 Edward VIII was on the throne, although he was to reign for just eleven months before abdicating to marry his true love, the twice-divorced Mrs Wallis Simpson. Unlike the King, who featured in this magazine, the 'Lovely Jumper' on the cover, with its simple patterning, was going to last. It is billed as the ideal top for spring weather, and it is suggested that it could also be worked in white, 'ideal for tennis or for the river'.

INSIDE · SPECIAL PHOTOGRAPH of
QUEEN MARY and HER GRANDCHILDREN
HOME JOURNAL
Vol. 5. No. 110.
April 11th, 1936.
Every Wednesday
3d

Knitting Instructions for this Lovely Jumper Inside

Scottish quality

In the 1930s, Scottish knitwear was regarded as the best in the world in terms of quality – although it was a little lacking in the fashion stakes. Pringle, one of the oldest manufacturers in the country, set about putting this right by being the first to appoint a designer, Otto Weiz. Pringle also claims to have invented the idea of the twin set, which would enjoy continued popularity for years to come. Even men would adopt them, though with a casual button-neck sweater rather than the round-collar version favoured by the ladies.

Underneath it all

Nobody today would consider knitting their own underwear, but in depressed times money is a much rarer commodity than time. These elegant vests show the influence of the 1920s in their styling, which isn't surprising because fashion transitions only happen overnight at catwalk level and take longer to reach the street. However, notice the ribbing at the waist. This is a feature on

BESTWAY LEAFLET **3ᵈ** No. 758

VEST in STOCKSIZE or OUTSIZE
4 ozs. and 5 ozs. of 3-ply

BESTWAY LEAFLET **3ᵈ** 1057

DAINTY VEST & KNICKERS
9 ozs. of 3-ply for Set

both vests as well as the knickers and helps to ensure the smooth lines of over-garments. Both patterns claim to stretch up to a 34in chest while the 'outsize' version available for the vest is suitable for a 36in chest, showing how slender the general population tended to be.

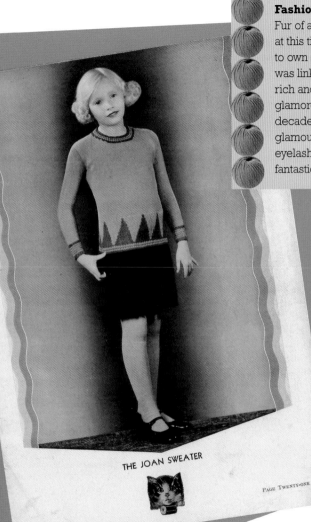

THE JOAN SWEATER

PAGE TWENTY-ONE

Youth style

What's interesting here is how stylish this little lady looks in her sweater. She is clearly fashion-conscious – or her parents are. It's easy to think that it wasn't until the 1960s that fashion touched youth, but clearly that isn't so.

The war-time '40s

During World War II, fabrics were in short supply. More synthetic fibres were developed and clothing styles used less fabric. Skirts were shorter and narrower, and so were jackets, and many more women now wore trousers. The idea of coordinating outfits came into being and ladies were encouraged to mix and match in order to give the impression of a greater number of outfits.

War work

Women were encouraged by the government to knit for the war effort, and millions of socks were made for soldiers. Free patterns were given away for utilitarian garments, including balaclavas with earflaps for radio operators, and mittens with a separate forefinger for pulling a trigger.

Make do and mend
Rationing brought wool into short supply in the UK, so the government produced a booklet entitled 'Make Do and Mend', which encouraged ladies to unpick old or unsuitable items and reuse the wool – something some people still like to do today. Despite the rationing, English women made huge efforts to keep up appearances and morale. They wore all sorts of hats, often knitted, to embellish their outfits and made many other items – knitted slippers and sandals were fashionable, for example, as well as knitted bags, sweaters and cardigans.

Beware of women bearing gifts

The idea that presents we have made ourselves will be as joyfully received as something brought from *iwantoneofthose.com* goes a long way back. Take a look at the natty little gift suggestions from this magazine, or show them to friends and loved ones as a warning of what might have been if they criticise the handknitted scarf you gave them.

Pick of the crop

If you thought that cropped tops were new, you'd be wrong – they've been around for decades. This fashion book from the 1940s, for example, features jackets that end just below the bust as well as boleros and shrugs designed to show off a slender figure.

The fabulous '50s

The same big fashion houses still dominated after the war, but they were producing new lines, and in 1947 Dior launched his 'New Look'. In the US, a film and teenage culture was developing – its impact on fashion design would eventually filter through to the rest of the world. Knitting still wasn't exactly rock 'n' roll, but there were signs...

Crop tops

Who would have thought that these scantily clad lovelies were photographed in 1952, when Dior was emphasizing the hourglass figure in chic suits and billowing skirts? If you saw either outfit today you wouldn't be surprised. The only difference is that a cropped top would now reveal cardio-flattened, fake-tanned abs complete with tattoos and piercings (just don't get them caught in the yarn – ouch).

A cropped top would now reveal fake-tanned abs

Plastic fantastic

Synthetic yarn is a product of the 1950s, not of the 1960s as often thought. In 1950, DuPont™ launched Orlon®, an acrylic yarn. Rival companies soon followed. No one has knitted fast enough to cause meltdown yet, but you never know...

Slinky sweaters

Until the 1950s, fashion was aimed at the mature, fully formed woman, but teens dressed in these styles just looked downright dowdy. Now fashions started to be designed especially for them. Judging by the picture, these turtleneck sweaters appear to have an alluring pulling power, and are described in the pattern's title as 'Hand Knits with Gracious Manners'. So take your cue from this era, sling on your slinkiest sweater and practise a politely coy glance – it should prove an irresistible combination.

Sling on your slinkiest sweater and practise a politely coy glance

Turtleneck Sweaters
Hand-Knits with Gracious Manners

TURTLENECK SWEATER WITH BEADS C-150

Illustrated on opposite page

Sizes 12, 14 and 16

Directions are given for Size 12.
Changes for Sizes 14 and 16 are in parentheses.

MATERIALS: CHADWICK'S RED HEART SOCK AND SWEATER YARN, 3 Ply. Shrink-and-Resist Finish, Art. E-255; 6 (6, 7) skeins (1 oz. "Tangle-Proof" Pull-Out Skeins) of No. 1 White . . . Milward's "Phantom" Aluminum Knitting Pins, 1 pair No. 1 (2½) mm. sizes; 1 pair No. 3 (3 mm. sizes) Needles or Clark's O.N.T. Aluminum Double-pointed Steel Needles, 1 set No. 1 (3 mm. size) . . . Clark's O.N.T. Plastic Crochet Hook No. 1.

GAUGE: 7 sts make 1 inch; 9 rows make 1 inch.

BLOCKING MEASUREMENTS: Bust—32 (34, 36) inches; Width across back or front at underarm—16 (17, 18) inches; Length from shoulder to lower edge—18 (18, 19) inches; Length of side seam—12 (12, 12½) inches.

BACK . . . Starting at lower edge, cast on 103 (109, 117) sts. Work in ribbing of k 1 (row), p 1 row) for 3 rows. Continue in stockinette st, slipping markers, until piece measures 1 inch, ending with a p row. Dec 1 st at both sides of center marker in every 10th row thereafter until there remain 87 (93, 101) sts. Work without decreasing until there remain 87 (93, 101) sts. Work without increasing until piece measures 11 (11½, 12, 12½) inches, ending with a p row. Place a marker at both ends of next row (start of top of sleeves).

CAP SLEEVES . . . Inc 1 st at both ends of next row and every 8th row thereafter until there are 20 rows. Work without increasing until sleeve measures 3 (3½, 3½) inches from sleeve markers.

To Shape Top of Sleeves and Shoulders: Bind off 3 sts at the beginning of next 8 (8, 10) rows. Bind off 4 to 6 sts (6, 6½) inches from sleeve markers.

FRONT . . . Work exactly as for Back until piece measures . . .

Continued on page 13

SLEEVELESS TURTLENECK SWEATER C-151

Illustrated on opposite page

Sizes 12, 14 and 16

Directions are given for Size 12.
Changes for Sizes 14 and 16 are in parentheses.

MATERIALS: CHADWICK'S RED HEART SOCK AND SWEATER YARN, 3 Ply. Shrink-and-Shetlk Resist Finish, Art. E-255; 6 (6, 7) skeins (1 oz. . . . Tangle-Proof Pull-out Skeins) of No. 848 Skipper Blue . . . Milward's "Phantom" Aluminum Knitting Pins or Clark's O.N.T. Plastic Knitting Pins, 1 pair No. 1 (2½) mm. sizes; Needles, or Clark's O.N.T. Plastic Double-pointed Steel Needles, 1 set No. 1 (2½) mm. size) . . . Clark's O.N.T. Plastic Crochet Hook No. 1.

GAUGE: 9 sts make 1 inch; 11 rows make 1 inch.

BLOCKING MEASUREMENTS: Bust—32 (34, 36) inches; Width across back or front at underarm—16 (17, 18) inches; Length from shoulder to lower edge—18½ (19½, 19½) inches; Length of side seam—11 (11, 11½) inches.

FRONT . . . Starting at lower edge, cast on 123 (129, 135) sts. Work in rib pattern as follows: **1st row:** K 3, * p 3, k 3. Repeat from * across. **2nd row:** p 3, * k 3, p 3. Repeat from * across. The last 2 rows constitute pattern. Keeping continuity of pattern, inc 1 st at both ends of every 8th row thereafter until there are 147 (153, 159) sts thereafter without decrease until piece measures 11 (11, 11½) inches. Place a work without measures at both ends (start armholes) . . . Work without increasing until piece measures from marker 5 (5, 5½) inches, ending with a 2nd row of pattern.

To Shape Neck: Work in pattern over the first 8 (9, 88) sts. Place the last 17 sts just worked on a stitch holder to be worked later for turtleneck. Work in pattern across . . .

Continued on page 13

French chic

Ladies who hankered after the elegant styles of the catwalk fashions could knit their own chic suits or dresses in the style of Christian Dior's 'New Look'. However, being worked at a gauge of 7½ stitches to the inch, with nearly 400 stitches round the skirt for even the smallest size, it would have taken a lot of dedication to complete this project.

Fifties fashion

Still not sure what 1950s fashion was all about? For teens, think of *Grease* – cashmere sweaters, pedal pushers, black leather jackets, rolled-up jeans and bobby socks with flat shoes. For the older look, think Debbie Reynolds and Audrey Hepburn – full shirts worn with cinch belts and classic shirts or narrow, figure-hugging slacks. All to be worn with neat leather gloves, hat and scarf.

58 Belted bathing

With the invention of Lycra, thank goodness knitted swimwear is history!

Don't get it wet…

The idea of knitted swimwear like this may seem ludicrous to us, but before the invention of Lycra there wasn't much choice. I for one would have liked to have been there when this chap stepped out of the water. No wonder it needed a belt…

49

> # Fashion is made to become unfashionable
>
> *Coco Chanel*

Duff stuff

Every era produces some rather unfortunate knitting patterns, and the 1950s were no exception. No wonder this model is wearing such a pained smile. Over-embellishment is never good, and here the cable-patterned scarf and hat are topped with large and small sequins and beads.

The joys of jersey

One of the most lauded fashion designers, Coco Chanel, pioneered the change in women's fashions from the restrictive towards the comfortable and created practical pieces in knitted jersey fabrics from the 1920s onwards. By the 1950s, jersey was thoroughly in fashion for tops, skirts and dresses. Today it is a mainstay of many modern designers, including Ghost.

Seductive in lace

This sexy little number is knitted in a cotton and rayon mix for easy care in a pretty leafy pattern that is surprisingly revealing. The lacy pattern was totally up-to-the-minute in the 1950s, as is the clinched waist and massively full skirt that took advantage of the sudden availability of fabric after the lean war-time years.

Full skirts took advantage of the sudden availability of fabric after the war

Flexible style

Here's an idea from the 1950s that could be modified to suit today's fashions. The extra-wide neck can be worn as a collar, across the shoulders or draped in interesting ways around the neck. Knitted up in one of the cuddly, funky yarns of today it could be transformed into a groovy casual/disco top.

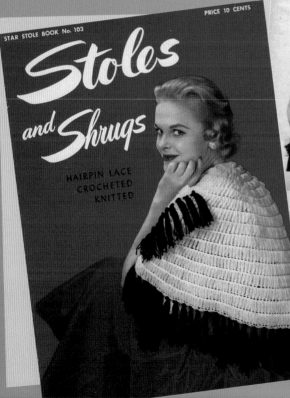

Shrug it off

'Stoles are the very essence of fashion', we are told, and 'made by smart women everywhere'. The cover design is worked in nylon, a new and exciting fibre, and though you may find it frankly revolting, some of the wraps and shrugs inside look suspiciously like the patterns of today.

The swinging '60s

This was the decade of youth, when the post-war baby-boomers were now teenagers. The mini skirt appeared, made possible by the introduction of tights in place of stockings, and was worn with court shoes or go-go boots. There were several basic looks, ranging from hippy style to an arty look inspired by the likes of the Beatles and David Bailey. Colours were usually bright and bold or neutral, and styles were generally skimpy – a bonus for the busy knitter.

New brights

Continued developments in synthetic yarns and dyes made brighter colours possible, and over the course of the decade they were to get even louder. The bold red ensemble on the front of this pattern book is a perfect example.

Cut above the rest
1966 was the year of the mini skirt, and every smart woman was wearing them. In New York the hemline rested 4–5in above the knee, but in London, under the influence of Mary Quant, 7–8in above the knee was more like it. However, you weren't really with it unless you had the matching skinny rib sweater and tights.

Sunbather

Ibiza was set to become
fashionable with the Germans
and British over the course of the
1960s and 1970s, and more people
started to go sun-seeking abroad.
This 'dashing little mini-top with
mini-shorts to match' was ideal for
such a holiday.

STYLE NO. 2187-109—Directions on page 28

STYLE NO. 2168-109—Directions on page 28

STYLE NO. 2180-109—Directions on page 29

STYLE NO. 2179-109—Directions on page 29

Bewitching?

The cult TV series *Bewitched* began in 1964.
Can't you just see Mother, a.k.a. Agnes
Moorehead/Shirley MacLaine in fetching
little numbers like these?

The arty '60s

The arty look was a dominant fashion of the 1960s – as in the black polo-neck sweaters and matching suits of the Beatles and the slightly jazzier look of contemporary artists such as Andy Warhol and David Hockney. David Bailey's black-and-white photographs of the stars of the day captured a quintessential 1960s look. Mary Quant was influential as the originator of the mini skirt. She designed knitwear too – her striped skinny rib sweater was seen everywhere.

Arty chic

This image shows the influences of David Bailey and Mary Quant – the pose is dynamic, and the clothing simple but striking. The dashing top is knitted in grey and mulberry red, and would have been an easy-to-wear classic.

> " *Fashion, as we knew it, is over; people wear now exactly what they feel like wearing.* "
>
> Mary Quant

Youth culture

In the 1960s young women didn't try to look mature any more – it was not only okay to be young, it was essential. Here's the original little-girl look of socks and skirt, now reinvented by Britney Spears.

Cosy coat

Here's English supermodel Twiggy in a chunky coat knitted up in thick and thin Bernat Klein wool. The coat wouldn't look out of place today, though the colour would be different, perhaps mottled or random dyed.

The hippy chic '70s

Tank tops and ponchos were the order of the day in the 1970s, along with long *Dr Who* scarves, denim bellbottoms, clogs or platform shoes and beads. Knitted dresses were also in favour, as were chunky, textured jumpers, made famous by *Starsky & Hutch*. Crafts such as macramé, crochet and knitting were in vogue, especially with the young. Natural materials tended to be used rather than synthetics. There was also an interest in the natural products of Africa and Asia – Afghan coats and cheesecloth were everywhere.

Acid blast

This is a prime example of the high fashion of the time. Knitted in a highly desirable acidic yellow mohair, the design has the type of ethnic feel that was all the rage at the time. The combination of tassels and lacy pattern captures the look of the Afghan coats and ponchos that were so much in style. Even the ankle-length finish of the skirt was up to the minute, and the natural material was a must. This was a teenage dream of the time.

2891

Emu

FILIGREE

23 to 29 inch
waist sizes

7½p
1/6

Top it all

The 1970s wouldn't have been the 1970s without tank tops, or without orange, beige and brown. These nifty fashion items provided a quick way of jazzing up an outfit and were relatively easy to knit. They were so popular in this era that nine of the patterns in this booklet are tank tops or waistcoats, including one for every member of the family.

Knitting in your lifestyle

Taken from a *Woman's Own* leaflet entitled 'Knitting in Your Lifestyle' these images show some typically 1970s knits. I'm afraid to say that I had an outfit like the one worn by the girl on the bicycle, and very smart I thought I looked too. Even worse, the girl in the bolero and skirt could have been my sister (who was much more fashion-oriented than me), though there was less of an age gap between us than that.

The booming '80s

The youth culture that dominated the 1960s and 1970s lost prominence in the 1980s when the Western economy boomed. In came the concept of power dressing – expensive skirt suits with shoulder-pads, perhaps teamed with a red shirt or something in satin. On the other side of the scale, headbands and legwarmers were in fashion, along with batwing sleeves, sunglasses and sharp looks. Sales of yarns and patterns took a nosedive. Knitting had been relegated from a useful occupation to a hobby and now it had been reduced to a kind of underground movement.

Guiding lights in the US

Make a search on the Internet for American knitting in the 1980s and it comes up with just one name – Elizabeth Zimmermann. Three of her books – *Knitter's Almanac*, *Knitting Around* and *Knitting Workshop* were all first printed in the 1980s and had a huge influence in the US. Other American knitwear luminaries of the time include Edina Ronay and Nicky Epstein – who is still producing fantastic knitting books today. In the 1980s, even fashion designers were getting in on the knitting act, with Perry Ellis, Adrienne Vittadini and Calvin Klein all creating designs for *Vogue Knitting International*.

For knitters, the 1980s was the start of the barren years. Readily available, inexpensive machine-knitted items meant there was no longer a financial reason to knit.

Hope in the UK

In the UK, Patricia Roberts was helming a knitting revolution, bringing the designer touch to home knitting and producing designs that were both unusual and challenging. At the same time Rowan, led by Stephen Sheard, came into being. Stephen took yarns to top professional designers and incorporated their views into developing the next batch. Soon Rowan was producing sought-after books of patterns with designs by such names as Kaffe Fassett, Artworks and Annabel Fox. These raised the standard of knitting patterns for the home knitter and began to gather an elite following.

Japanese style

Knitwear was still gracing the catwalks in the 1980s as a break from the shoulder pads and leggings. Here, design house Kenzo shows its fall–winter ready-to-wear line in Paris in 1984–1985.

Nightclub knits

Although the 1980s in general were not knitwear's finest hour, some people managed to make innovations in knitted style. Here, some nightclubbers pose in their fabulous knitted creations.

Pearl to perfection

Synthetic yarns were used extensively in the 1980s because easy-care clothes had become important to the working woman and because these yarns tended to be cheaper than natural fibres. Space dyeing was popular as a means of adding patterning, enabling knitters to add colour to their garments quickly and easily in their limited hobby time. The batwing pattern shown here was up-to-the-minute, as was its pearly space-dyed fluffy acrylic yarn in a chunky size for fast completion.

689

Argyll

Fluffy One & Fluffy Chunky

76–102 cm.
30–40 ins.

Speed knit

Mottled and flecked yarns were in fashion in the 1980s because they provided colour, texture and pattern quickly and effortlessly. The concept of quick and easy was more important than ever, and this is one of a series of patterns that was highlighted as being one of a range of 'speed knits'. Patterns tended to be simpler than ever, and this top has an easy boat neck.

Lister
Handknitting

BAMBOO
5044
30-38 in (76-97 cm)

SPEED KNITS

Stripe me pink

Everything about this image is thoroughly 1980s, from the bold colour combination and loud zigzag patterns of the sweaters to the soft focus of the photography. Design was about experimenting with the new – notice the unusual neck design of the black sweater and the bold decision to combine patterns in colour and texture. This pattern is by Patricia Roberts, one of the leading lights in knitting design who helped to get knitting back in the fashion stakes.

End of a century

At the start of the 1990s, knitting was dead for most of us. You could buy a readymade sweater for less than the cost of the yarn, and a lack of demand meant it was harder and harder to find suppliers. However, this was also when things started to turn around. New designers had arrived to give knitting a whole new desirability, including Kaffe Fassett, with his luscious colour combinations, Kate Buller with her gorgeous intarsia patterns, and Kim Hargreaves and Louisa Harding, who brought out the true qualities of natural fibres through the use of texture. The handknit look was making a comeback.

Simply desirable

Simplicity was one of the themes of 1990s knitting, as captured in the designs of Kim Hargreaves and others. She brought out the natural qualities of the yarn with simple patterning and styling. The designs made you feel you could almost sense the qualities of the yarn without even touching it.

Colour rich

Kaffe Fassett combined intense colours with often complicated patterning in his knitwear designs for an effect of mouth-watering lusciousness. His knits simply had to be handmade – there was no other way – and that was part of their desirability.

LEFT: Vibrant colours, simple stitches and chunky yarn are key features of much contemporary fashion knitwear, as shown in this jumper by Junko Shimada.

Sheer bliss

No coverage of 1990s knitting would be complete without discussing Debbie Bliss. She brought the desirability back into children's knitwear and got even the young and trendy bringing out the needles to make something for a nephew or niece.

RIGHT: Fashion's top names began to see the potential of using knitwear in their collections: this ultra-chic two-piece knitted suit is by John Galliano.

Knits of the nineties

Some of the most fashionable knits of the 1980s were fashioned in Fair Isle designs or featured ornate intarsia picture patterns. In contrast, the knits of the 1990s tended to be plain, though perhaps using textural designs for interest. Towards the middle of the decade, patterning was back around neck and cuff, and by the end of the decade Fair Isle was in fashion again, showing that you can't keep a good knitting pattern down.

21st-century knits

Revival is the key word here. The growing interest in knitting that had begun in the late 1990s continued. As demand for patterns and yarns increased, the manufacturers quickly recognized a widening market and started putting new, exciting yarns on the market. It was a yarn Renaissance. Special attention was given to stunning novelty yarns, and companies like Rowan produced ever-more exciting designs that rivalled catwalk images. No longer was knitting a dull, domestic issue – it was an aspect of high fashion, made more desirable by the participation of the superstars. These days, knitwear design and yarn manufacture is expanding and transforming all the time, and this may be only the beginning.

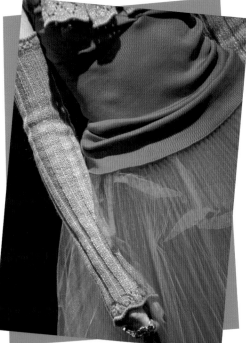

Knitted bits

A big item in the early 21st century is the knitted accessory, especially for the young. US hip knitting show *Knitty Gritty* has included such funky items as knitted cozies for MP3 players and guitar straps, for example, while the Cast Off group in the UK offers knitting kits for making such unusual items as knitted shoelaces, blindfolds and cigarettes (for those who can't quite give up). Patterns for purses and bags of all types are widely circulated and you can even knit your own necklaces and other jewellery (see Lion Brand, for example).

RIGHT: These funky armwarmers by Stella Cadente are typical of a new generation of fabulous knitted accessories.

Catwalk influences

Knitwear used to be pretty much invisible on the catwalk – it was there but normally just to back up the other clothing, and only knitwear designers took much notice. Luckily, times are changing. Issey Miyake, Yohji Yamamoto, Missoni, Comme des Garçons and Vivienne Westwood are cutting-edge designers who have all used knitwear to express their fashion ideals and even more conservative designers such as Betty Jackson, Joseph and Chanel show it consistently as part of their collections. Actually, some fabulous or wild and wacky knitwear designs have been on the catwalk since the 1980s, but it has taken a while for us poor folks on the streets to get the designs. The good news is that now pattern designers know that there is such a market for up-to-the-minute knitwear designs they should be filtering through to us much, much faster. Just watch the innovative yarn and pattern designers and you'll soon see.

RIGHT: Extraordinary modern yarns are used to stunning effect in this loosely knit blue dress.

> *Nowadays you don't have to be rich to have beautiful things.*
> Karl Lagerfeld

Lacolourful Lacoste

Lacoste give their classic sportswear-influenced designs a fresh look with some eye-popping modern colours.

Viva Vivienne

Acclaimed British designer Vivienne Westwood has long used knitwear with an eccentric twist in her innovative collections

Last of the yarn

Aftercare

Whether it's taken you hours, days, weeks, months or years to knit your creation, you won't want it to shrink or distort out of shape after the first wash. Don't do what I always do and throw away the yarn label, because you won't have the invaluable washing instructions on the back. You'll have a lot of hand washing in front of you, too.

The care label on the ball will tell you if your yarn is machine-washable and machine-dryable, if it's hand wash only and if you can iron it (though why anyone would want to iron a woolly is beyond me). Believe it or not, some modern yarns are actually dry clean only, so look out for this too (see opposite). In fact, I would recommend reading the care label before you buy the yarn in order to avoid a precious knit moulding away in the wash basket for weeks at a time because you intend to 'wash it tomorrow'.

Hand washing

If your woolly does need hand washing, it's really not such a big deal. Buy a liquid detergent suitable for woollens, silks and other delicates and mix the required amount in a bucket of warm water – bath temperature. At this point I dunk my jumper, hat or whatever in the bowl, squeeze it to make sure the water is penetrating and then go and do something more interesting. When I remember the woolly I come back, give it a few more squeezes and then rinse it thoroughly in cool water. If you are aware of any particular marks or stains, you should give these a gentle rub. Small items can be squeezed to get most of the water out and then dried flat – never hang a wet woollen or it will stretch magnificently out of shape. Larger items are more of a problem. If you possess a mangle/wringer or spin dryer then you can use it briefly to get rid of excess water. Otherwise, keep squeezing the item, then wrap it in a towel and squeeze again. Dry it flat.

Machine washing

If your yarn is machine washable, you have no problem. Do not, however, exceed the stated maximum temperature – usually 40°C or 104°F – and set the machine to a short or special woollen wash, which has minimum agitation. Hot water and agitation combine to give excellent felting results, so if you don't want to felt or shrink your woolly then avoid them. Of course, if your jumper is too big you could try a hot wash to shrink it down to size – or give it to a fatter friend with good will.

Steamy solution

Avoid ironing your woollens if at all possible. If a jumper is creased, hang it in the bathroom while you have a bath or shower – the steam should release the creases.

Storage

Storage is more of an issue for woollies than for synthetic, cotton or even silk knits. However, whatever the fibre, you should never hang knitted garments because they will stretch out of shape and the hanger may damage the shoulders of dresses or sweaters. Instead, fold and store them flat. For woollens, take account of the following guidelines:

Washing symbols

Here are the standard symbols you'll find on yarn labels and what they mean.

Use mothballs, crystals or sprays to protect precious woollens from moth attacks.

Store clean woollens in sealed paper garment bags over the summer months as an extra moth-proofing precaution.

If you can afford one, buy a camphor wood chest for storage: this wood is a natural moth repellent and you won't have to bother with stinky mothballs.

Make sure woollens are clean before you put them away – dirt seems to attract insects and mould spores.

 Hand wash using water up to 40°C or 104°F

 Machine wash with water up to 40°C or 104°F

 Machine dry but on a gentle setting

 Do not machine dry

 You may use chlorine bleach

 Do not use bleach

 Iron press if needed

 Do not press

 Dry clean

Do not dry clean

Dry clean using P solvents only

Shows, groups, resources

If you want to learn to knit, brush up on your techniques, find out about the latest yarns, get a yarn bargain or meet fellow knitters, go to a yarn fair or show or join a group. If you can get on the Internet, this is the place to find out about events in your area, or buy a knitting magazine produced in your country and scan through the ads.

Links in the UK

The **Knitting and Stitching Show,** held in London, Dublin and Harrogate, hosts more than 100 workshops and at least 300 stands. For further information, go to *www.twistedthread.com* or phone 01473 320407.

Stitches and Hobbycrafts at Exeter, Cardiff, Brighton and Glasgow includes a 'knit 'n' natter' section with experts on hand to give advice. For further information, go to *www.ichf.co.uk* or call 01425 272711.

To find a knitting group near you try the following:

Knitchicks *www.knitchicks.co.uk*

British Knitting and Crochet Guild, which also lists a large number of knitting events *www.bhkc. co.uk*

Stitch n Bitch *www.stitchnbitch.org* – go the UK or Ireland categories.

Magazines

Knitting *www.thegmcgroup.com*. The Guild of Master Craftsmen, 166 High Street, Lewes, East Sussex BN7 1XU.
Tel: 01273 488005

Simply Knitting Unit 4, Tower House, Sovereign Park, Market Harborough, Leicestershire LE16 9EF.
Tel: 0870 837 4722

Rowan Magazines
www.knitrowan.com

Links in the US

Knit-Out and Crochet organized by the Yarn Council of America held in New York, Pasadena CA, Washington DC, Charlotte NC, and many more venues. For further information, go to *www.craftyarncouncil.com*

Stitches events including Stitches West, Stitches Midwest, Camp Stitches and Stitches East. For further information, go to *www.knittinguniverse.com*

To find a knitting group near you, try the following:
Meetup *www.knitting.meetup.com*
Menknit *www.menknit.net*
Stitch n Bitch *www.stitchnbitch.org*

Magazines

Vogue Knitting International
www.vogueknitting.com

Knit.1 *www.vogueknitting.com*

Interweave Knits *www.interweave.com*

Creative Knitting
www.creativeknittingmagazine.com

MenKnit (online only) *www.menknit.net*

Stitches (online only) *www.knittinguniverse.com*

Knitty (online only) *www.knitty.com*

Contacts

A Few Good Blogs

Kerry's site (see page 38) *www.kerriesplace.co.uk*
Queer Joe's blog spot *www.queerjoe.blogspot.com*
Stephanie Pearl McPhee, author of *At Knit's End*
www.yarnharlot.ca/blog/

Shopping

Angel Yarns
Comprehensive yarn supplies, including hand-dyed wools and silks plus wonderful stitch markers and other accessories; based in the UK.
www.yarn-shop.co.uk

Camilla Valley Farm Weavers' Supply
Lopi yarn, cotton yarn and equipment; based in Canada. *www.camillavalleyfarm.com*

Caron
Manufacturers of basic and high-fashion yarns; based in the US. *www.lornalaces.net*

Coats Crafts
Manufacturer of standard and fashion yarns; based in the US. *www.coats.com* or in the UK *www.coatscrafts.co.uk*

Colinette Yarns
Very modern and unusual yarns in various fibres, kits and ideas; based in the UK. *www.colinette.com*

Get Knitted
Large range of yarns, kits and patterns, including unusual and ecological brands; based in the UK. *www.getknitted.com*

Kaleidoscope Yarns
Comprehensive yarn supplies including most leading brands; based in the US. *www.kaleidoscopeyarns.com*

Kangaroo
Leading-brand yarns including Noro and Debbie Bliss; based in the UK. *www.kangaroo.co.uk*

Knit Knack
Stunning knitting cases and even more glorious needles to go in them – ideal for the knitter who has everything; based in the US. *www.knitknack.com*

Lantern Moon
Some of the most beautiful knitting needles you will ever see; based in the US. *www.lanternmoon.com.* Available in the UK from *www.purlescence.co.uk*, along with other desirables.

Laughing Hens
Wide selection of yarns and patterns and lovely buttons; based in the UK. *www.laughinghens.com*

Lion Brand
Yummy wools and a massive array of free fashionable patterns; based in the US. *www.lionbrand.com*

Lorna's Laces
Unusual hand-dyed yarn in natural fibres; based in the US. *www.lornaslace.net*

Patons Yarns
Leading yarn manufacturer, based in the US but yarns available everywhere (in the UK go to *www.coatscrafts.co.uk*) *www.patonsyarns.com*

Rowan Yarns
Quality British yarns and wonderful pattern books; based in the UK. *www.knitrowan.com*

Sirdar
Leading yarn manufacturer; based in the UK. *www.sirdar.co.uk*

Sweater Babe
Funky patterns, tips and classes; based in the US. *www.sweaterbabe.com*

Wool Works
Free patterns and advice; based in Canada. *www.woolworks.org*

Yarn Market
Massive range of yarns, kits, books, projects and more; based in the US. *www.yarnmarket.com*

Acknowledgments

Many thanks to everyone at David & Charles for getting me involved with this book and especially Jennifer Proverbs for her lively enthusiasm and encouragement. Special thanks go to Prudence Rogers for her fantastic book design. Thanks also to Julien for helping me with the quiz and for his support and encouragement and to Sebastian for being himself.

The publishers would like to thank Jenny Hill for the loan of her amazing vintage knitting pattern library.

About the author

Betsy Hosegood is a keen crafter who has been knitting since her teens. She graduated with an MA in English from St Andrews University, Scotland, and has spent her working life crafting, editing and writing books. She lives in idyllic Devon with partner Julien and son Sebastian, and an ever-increasing range of pets and animals.

Picture acknowledgments

The pictures used in this book have come from many sources and acknowledgment has been made wherever possible. If images have been used without due credit or acknowledgment, through no fault of our own, apologies are offered. If notified the publisher will be pleased to rectify any errors or ommisions in future editions.

p1, p25, p117 Mel Yates/Getty Images; p5, p46 © Corbis; p6 Ericka McConnell/Getty Images; p11 Fox Photos/Getty Images; p12 Fox Photos/Getty Images; p14–15 © Underwood & Underwood/Corbis; p16 © Lucidio Studio Inc./Corbis; p18 © Anna Peisl/zefa/Corbis; p19 Martin Barraud ; p20 © Bettmann/Corbis; p21 Helena Inkeri/Getty Images; p22 Julia Fullerton-Batten/Getty Images; p23 © Anna Peisl/zefa/Corbis; p24 © Larry Williams/Corbis; p27 Giantstep Inc./Getty Images; p28 © Ronnie Kaufman/Corbis; p32 © Emely/zefa/Corbis; p36 Deborah Jaffe/Getty Images; p50 Bob Elsdale/Getty Images; p51 (left) Phil Schofield/Getty Images, (right) Kevin Schafer/Getty Images; p52 (top) © Kurt Kormann/zefa/Corbis, (bottom) © Yann Arthus-Bertrand/Corbis; p53 © Lance Nelson/Stock Photos/zefa/Corbis; p55 Mark Scott/Getty Images; p57 © Jon Feingersh/zefa/Corbis; p72 © Emely/zefa/Corbis; p74 © Katy Winn/Corbis; p75 © Robert Galbraith/Reuters/Corbis; p76 © Corbis; p77 © Getty Images Images; p79 © Lucy Nicholson/Reuters/Corbis; p83 © Pablo Corral V/Corbis; p85 *Home Journal*, 11 April 1936, © The Amalgamated Press Ltd.; p86 (both pictures) Bestway Leaflet No. 758, © The Amalgamated Press Ltd.; p87 *Men's and Children's Knitted Wear*, Booklet No. YP 52, © Belding-Corticelli Limited; p89 (both pictures) *Modern Needlecraft*, No. 29; p90–93 *Vogue Knitting*, Spring and Summer 1952, © Condé Nast Publications; p93 *Coats and Clark's Mittens and Accessories*, Book No. 316, © Coats & Clark Inc., 1955; p94 *Cool Hand Knits* Vol. 158, © Bernhard Ulmann Co. Inc., 1955; p95 (top) *Knitting by Anny Blatt de Paris*, © Tendances Inc.; p95 (bottom) *Star Stole Book* No. 103, © The American Thread Company, 1953; p96 *Stitchcraft* February 1969, © Condé Nast Publications Ltd.; p97 (left) *Caps and Mittens for Everybody from Bernat*, book 109, © Emile Bernat & Sons Co., 1962; p97 (right) *Four Seasons* No. 152, © Patons & Baldwins Limited; p98 and p99 (top) *Vogue Knitting* No. 69, © Condé Nast Publications Ltd; p99 (bottom) *Woman* 14 October 1967, © Odhams Press Ltd., 1967; p100 Emu 2891, © Emu Wools Ltd.; p101 (top and bottom) *Knitting in your Lifestyle* (free with *Woman's Own* 27 March 1971); p103 (left) © Corbis, (right) © Pierre Vauthey/Corbis Sygma; p104 Argyll 689, © Argyll Wools Ltd.; p105 (left) Lister Handknitting Bamboo 5044, © Lister Handknitting, (right) *Another 20 Patricia Roberts Knitting Patterns*, © Macdonald and Jane's Ltd., 1976; p106 © Orban Thierry/Corbis Sygma; p107 © Orban Thierry/Corbis Sygma; p108 © Orban Thierry/Corbis Sygma; p109 © Orban Thierry/Corbis Sygma; p110 (left) © Scott McDermott/Corbis (right) © Daniele La Monaca/Reuters/Corbis; p111 © Getty Images Images; p114 © Grace/zefa/Corbis.

Index

acrylics 53, 90, 104
aftercare 114–15
ages, today's knitters 73
alpaca 51
Andean style 82
angora 52
Arquette, David 73, 74

bamboo yarn 52
benefits of knitting 6–7, 18–23, 36
Bliss, Debbie 82, 107
blogs 16–17, 28, 38, 116, 118
bobble yarns & bouclés 64
brain power 21, 23, 76

cafés 26
care labels 114
cashmere 52
Cast Off group 26, 108
celebrity knitters 15, 20, 74–9
charity knitting 22, 76, 78
chenilles 64
Chiengora 64
chunky yarns 32, 64, 106
concentration 21, 23, 76
cotton 53
Cox, Courtney 74
creativity 6–7, 18, 35, 82
crop tops 89, 90
Crowe, Russell 77
cutting technique 35

designers (fashion houses) 85, 92, 93, 96,
     98, 103, 107, 109–111
designers (knitwear) 28, 82, 85, 102, 106,
     107, 108
Diaz, Cameron 15, 75
disasters & mistakes 17, 37, 44, 45
dog yarn 64
dyeing 63

ethical yarns 66
eyelash yarns 65, 87

Fair Isle 35, 42, 43, 82, 107
fake furs 65, 87
Fassett, Kaffe 14–15, 33, 76, 82, 102, 106
feelings about knitting 4–7, 18, 24, 37–45
felting 42, 43, 115
fibres 50–53, 58
film knits 26
fine yarns 34–5, 62
finger roll test 61
Fox, Annabel 102
furs, fake 65, 87
gauge 35, 44, 45

groups 21, 25, 29
Gurnseys (ganseys) 13, 82

Halliwell, Geri 20, 77
Hannah, Daryl 75
hats 10, 33, 44, 88, 97
Hawn, Goldie 23, 75
Herzigova, Eva 78
history 10–13, 84–111

inhale test 61
inspirations & influences 82
intarsia 35, 107
Internet 16–17, 28, 38–9, 54, 56, 116–19

Jason's yarn 40–41
jersey 93
Jones, Catherine Zeta 77

Kerrie's yarn 38–9
Kitt, Eartha 76
knit cafés 26
knit-ins & knit-outs 26
knitted accessories 88, 93, 108
     see also specific types (eg hats)
knitting accessories 69
knitting frames 4, 13

learning to knit 20, 32–5, 36, 37–45
Lee, William 4, 13
linen 52
loft 61
Lopi yarn 50

Madonna 20, 75
male knitters 40–41, 44–5, 73
medium-weight yarns 62
Michael's yarn 44–5
mixing yarns 62
mohair 51, 100

needles 13, 68–9
     circular 7, 15, 33
nylon 53, 95

online shopping 28, 38–9, 54, 56, 118–19
organic yarns 66

Parker, Mary-Louise 78
patterns 15, 28, 32, 33, 38, 58, 73, 76, 88
     '30s 84–7
     '40s 13, 88–9
     '50s 90–95
     '60s 96–9
     '70s 100–101
     '80s 102–5, 107
     '90s 106–7
     21st century 108–111
personal stories 37–45

polyester 53
public knitting 7, 21, 26

quiz 46–7

rag-style yarns 65
rayon 53
relaxation see stress reduction
repetitive strain injury 37
Roberta's yarn 42–3
Roberts, Julia 75, 77, 79
Roberts, Patricia 102, 105
rope ladder escape 69
Rowan yarns 102, 108

Salima's yarn 37
sari silk 66
shopping 28, 38–9, 54–6, 118–19
shrugs & shawls 95, 100
silk 52, 66
skin test 61
social knitting 7, 21, 25–9, 36
socks, stockings & hose 10, 34, 45, 88
soy 52
space-dyed yarns 104
squeeze test 61
Stewart, Martha 14, 22, 76
storage 115
stress reduction 6, 19, 21, 22–3, 24, 75
Swank, Hilary 79
swatch cards 56
swimwear 92, 97
synthetic yarns 53, 90, 96, 104

tank tops 101
tape yarns 67
textured knits 13, 34, 82, 107
textured yarns 64–7, 105
thick & thin yarns 67, 99, 109
Thurman, Uma 15, 78
twin sets 85

underwear 86

viscose 53

washing 114–15
wool 50

yarns
     beginners 32, 34–5
     choosing and buying 28, 38–9, 54–6,
          58–61, 118–19
     varieties & fibres 7, 15, 50–53, 58, 62–7

Zimmermann, Elizabeth 13, 14–15, 17, 18,
     35, 50, 102